T5-AXI-494

CONSUMER GUIDE®

Baby Equipment Buying Guide

Author: Sandy Jones, M.A., has written numerous articles for national magazines on consumer issues affecting infants. Her book, *Good Things for Babies*, has served as a sourcebook of safety and consumer advice for parents for almost a decade.

Cover Photo Credits: Aprica Juvenile Products Division of Merchants Corporation of America; Century Products, Inc.; Cosco Inc.; Evenflo Juvenile Furniture Company; Graco Children's Products, Inc.; Little Tikes; Williamsburg/Connor, a Division of Connor Forest Industries Inc.

CONTENTS

INTRODUCTION

You're expecting a child! It's an exciting time in your life as you get ready to take on the responsibility, enjoyment, and changes that a new baby brings. But you also begin to realize that this is not just a time of anticipation, it is also a time of *preparation*. You want to bring your newborn home to an environment that is safe, comfortable, stimulating, and adequate.

The Editors of *Consumer Guide*®, with the advice of numerous baby experts, have prepared the **Baby Equipment Buying Guide,** a book designed to help you choose the best products for your new baby. Our recommendations give you the assurance of **safety, quality,** and **economy.**

Before you begin shopping for baby equipment, remember, it usually doesn't pay in the long run to buy the least expensive product. The cheapest stroller at the store may have thin metal bars that will bend and break with normal use. Seat belts may fray and latches may loosen. Poorly constructed wheels may wobble and then fall off. Most parents find that shopping for products that are moderately priced—neither top of the line nor the cheapest model—usually assures that the product is sturdy and durable.

SECOND-HAND PRODUCTS

While the U.S. Consumer Product Safety Commission and the Juvenile Products Manufacturers Association do their parts in aiding the consumer at the manufacturers' level, there is no real way to govern the quality of products purchased at garage sales or flea markets, or those products passed between family and friends. Even though it feels good to get a bargain, the truth is that you are better off to buy fewer items at a retail store than many items at a garage sale and take a chance with product safety.

Car restraints may not meet federal safety standards, toys may have paint containing lead or parts and pieces that are too small, old playpens may have mesh that is too wide or hinges that are exposed—any number of hazards may be posed. Your child's safety is worth more to you than the money you might save with older, used products.

USING THIS BOOK

The products that we have included in the **Baby Equipment Buying Guide** have been checked for availability; unfortunately we cannot account for product distribution across the entire United States. If you are unable to locate a product that we have recommended, we suggest that you write the manufacturer (see "Manufacturers Directory" at the back of the book) and ask for the location of a store near you that would carry the product. Also, all of the prices are accurate at the time of printing, but we have no control over price fluctuations.

It is important to note that prices will vary from store to store (and sometimes from state to state). The prices we have used are the prices that were available to us. We recommend that when possible you shop around for the best available price in your area. The price can vary a great deal between a discount store and a specialty shop.

From chapter to chapter, products are listed in alphabetical order. *They are not listed in the order of preference.* We believe that each of the products that we have recommended in the **Baby Equipment Buying Guide** is a good product; since needs vary from consumer to consumer, so do the possibilities of our products. Therefore we can't choose one as the "Best Buy" when the product that follows may be of just as high quality, but has an advantage that might appeal to the needs of another consumer. The Editors of *Consumer Guide*® believe all of the products we are recommending are products that are safe, economical, and of high quality.

A "Feature Checklist" is found in most of the chapters that follow. Some of the qualities that we recommend you shop for are a matter of safety; others are a matter of convenience. Our recommendation is that you *always* look for safety features when shopping, but convenience features are a matter of life-style.

SAFETY FIRST

Because babies are vulnerable, they need protection. When many parents buy baby equipment, they assume that since it is *designed* for babies, it is *safe* for babies. In fact, statistics gathered by the National Electronic Injury Surveillance System (NEISS) for the Consumer Product Safety Commission show that many baby products are actually harmful to them.

In the six-year period from 1979 through 1984, over 46,000 babies were treated in emergency rooms for crib-related injuries alone. Nearly 43,000 stroller-related injuries serious enough to require emergency room treatment were estimated between 1980 and 1984. In *one year* there were 23,000 walker-related injuries.

For many years, parents felt at fault when a baby's high chair collapsed, a baby's finger got cut in a playpen hinge, or a small piece of toy got stuck in a baby's throat. But now protective legislation is putting much of the responsibility on manufacturers.

U.S. CONSUMER PRODUCT SAFETY COMMISSION

The Consumer Product Safety Commission is an independent regulatory agency of the U.S. government and has the task of administering the laws and regulations concerning product safety—baby products as well as many other types of products. Since 1973 when the CPSC was created, an estimated 325 million potentially hazardous products have been called back from the marketplace. In most instances, the manufacturers voluntarily offered to recall, repair, or refund the purchase price of the product to the consumer.

The Consumer Product Safety Commission has a toll-free telephone number that you may call if you have questions or information about baby products: **1-800-638-CPSC.**

JUVENILE PRODUCTS MANUFACTURERS ASSOCIATION

The Juvenile Products Manufacturers Association (JPMA) is a national industry association made up of more than 100 companies that manufacture baby furniture and accessories. These manufacturers inaugurated a voluntary product certification program for high chairs, playpens, and strollers and carriages.

The American Society for Testing and Materials—an independent group—was asked by JPMA to develop standards for product safety. Once a product has passed their tests, the JPMA label may be applied to production models that meet their safety standards. Every year the manufacturers are required to resubmit their products for testing to assure that they still meet the certification requirements. This seal tells the consumer that the product was designed and built by a manufacturer who is concerned about the safety of children. The Editors of *Consumer Guide®* recommend that you look for this seal before purchasing a high chair, playpen, stroller, or carriage. This is what the seal looks like:

REGULATORY STANDARDS

The Consumer Product Safety Commission administers *laws;* manufacturers of products covered by these regulations *must* meet these requirements in order to sell their products. The most successful protective measures are those governing the *manufacture* of a product rather than those measures that simply require *warnings* asking parents to take some action to protect their babies from a product. Some of the best known and most effective regulations cover:
  Child-resistant caps for medicine bottles
  Control of lead paint
  Mandatory car restraints

Regulation of small parts and pieces on toys and pacifiers
Crib safety
Sleepwear for children

VOLUNTARY STANDARDS

Although federal regulations oversee the safety of car restraints, cribs, walkers, pacifiers, and certain toys for infants, there is a whole range of products that have either no standards or that come under the voluntary standards created by the Juvenile Products Manufacturers Association. *Voluntary* means that manufacturers are not forced to follow a safety standard.

And, parents should understand that in some cases, the voluntary standards are flawed. For example, a number of deaths have occurred in mesh-sided playpens when the sides have been left down with a baby in the playpen. (The child becomes entrapped in the pocket created by the loose mesh, and suffocates.) Currently only a warning is required to be posted on the playpen. Warnings generally have a weak effect on consumers.

Similarly, babies die from falls in strollers, yet the stroller standard simply specifies that units come with a restraining belt; no mention is made regarding the quality of the belt material or the latch. The test of the safety belt consists of tugs on an infantlike mannequin placed in the stroller (a test that lasts less than one minute). This certainly overlooks the dynamic nature of infant body movements.

FEATURE CHECKLIST

When shopping for baby products, keep the following in mind:

☐ **Safety Belts.** Look for good safety belts and buckles on products that have them. *Always* be sure to use them with your baby. Buckles should be easy enough for you to undo in a hurry, but difficult enough that the baby can't unbuckle it.

☐ **Avoid Sharp Hardware.** Inspect the inside and outside of the product to be sure that there are no sharp edges or harmful bolts or nuts that might hurt a baby.

☐ **Avoid Dangerous Hinges.** Examine collapsible products that have tubes creating an X-joint. These joints can crush small fingers unless the manufacturer has built in a separation between the bars so that they don't actually have contact with each other.

☐ **Check Stability.** Any products that are made to *hold* baby (chairs, seats, strollers, cribs, playpens) should be stable. There should be no danger of collapsing or tipping over with baby in them.

☐ **Sturdiness.** Inspect each product carefully for sturdiness and quality of materials. Shake cribs, rattle strollers, pinch vinyl, look at seams; compare one product to another.

- ☐ **Prices.** Once you have decided on a specific brand, compare prices at a variety of stores. Prices on car seats, for example, can vary as much as $10.
- ☐ **Returns.** Keep your receipts in a safe place. Write the complete name and model number of the purchased product on the back of the receipt. Get the name and address of the manufacturer from the packaging. If a product does not perform as it should with normal use, take it back to the store where you made the purchase. If the store manager is not cooperative, call the public relations director of the manufacturer to get instructions for getting a replacement part—or a replaced product.
- ☐ **Don't Overshop.** Resist the urge to run out and buy all of the products that catch your eye. Buy products only when you're sure your baby will use them. Before making a purchase, divide the price of the product by the number of months your baby will be using it. Then decide whether it's a necessity or a luxury item.

And finally, a word from the Editors of *Consumer Guide*® to you—the new parent or the parent-to-be. While the products we have recommended are safe, high-quality items, they are not substitute parents. Never leave your baby unattended. All baby products should be used under watchful supervision.

CRIBS

Cribs, like most pieces of furniture, come in a variety of finishes and styles, from contemporary to traditional. And while you can choose an ornate model with a decorative carved headboard and fancy spindles, it is more economical to select a simple, functional crib that is sturdy enough to hold up for the two years or so that your baby will use it.

Prior to 1974, cribs were the least safe of all baby equipment. Since that time, federal safety standards have been established that mandate the following for any crib shipped in the United States:

Interior Dimensions. Your crib frame must measure 28 inches wide and 52⅜ inches long (give or take ⅝ inch) to ensure a firm fit between the crib and a standard-size crib mattress. By doing this, the crib mattress will fit securely inside the crib and eliminate a gap between the end of the mattress and the end of the crib. Otherwise, very young babies can trap their heads in this gap, causing strangulation.

Drop Side Position. There should be at least 9 inches between the mattress support in its highest position and the top of the drop side (the side that goes up and down) while in its lowest position. A baby could tumble out of the crib if the side is too low.

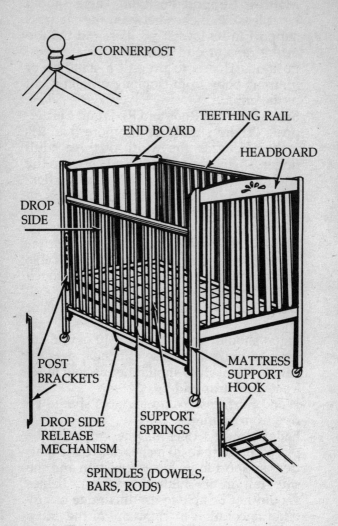

CORNERPOST

TEETHING RAIL

END BOARD

HEADBOARD

DROP SIDE

POST BRACKETS

MATTRESS SUPPORT HOOK

DROP SIDE RELEASE MECHANISM

SUPPORT SPRINGS

SPINDLES (DOWELS, BARS, RODS)

Mattress Support Position. There should be at least 26 inches between the mattress support in its lowest position and the top of the rails or end panels in their highest position. This is to prevent a standing or jumping baby from climbing or falling out of the crib.

Space Between Rods and Rods and Cornerposts. There should be no more than 2⅜ inches (roughly the width of three adult fingers) between each rod and between the end rod and the cornerposts. A baby's flexible body could slip through the railings on some cribs, leaving his neck wedged between the bars, causing strangulation.

Hardware. Screws, clamps, and other metal devices on the crib should be not able to cut, pinch, or bruise when babies touch or fall against them.

Drop Side Latching Device. The locking or latching device that holds the drop side railing(s) should require at least 10 pounds of force to make it release. Siblings, pets, or babies themselves should not be able to release the drop side.

Wood Surfaces. Wood surfaces should be free from splinters.

Ledges. Any ledges on the crib must be placed more than 20 inches above the mattress support in its lowest position and the side rail in its highest position. Babies should not be able to use this ridge or any other decoration to climb out of the crib.

Manufacturer's Instructions. Any crib that

is shipped unassembled should have clear, detailed instructions for assembly. There should also be warnings about keeping the bolts safely fastened once the crib is in use, and a warning that the crib should not be used by children over 35 inches tall. A crib that is incorrectly assembled could break or the hardware could bend, causing injury to the child. And, a child could be hurt attempting to climb out of a crib that he has outgrown.

Safety should be your main concern in purchasing baby furniture. Even with the stringent federal regulations that we have described, crib accidents continue to hurt babies. In 1984, more than 8,400 babies were injured seriously enough to be taken to hospital emergency rooms.

CHOOSING A CRIB

Your newborn may not need a crib right away. You may want to keep him in a bassinet or portable crib in your room so that you can hear him at night. In fact you may want to consider buying a smaller, portable, wheeled crib so that you can move your sleeping baby around the house.

One manufacturing innovation worth investigating is cribs that convert into twin- or full-sized beds. Even though these cribs are more expensive, they offer the extra advantage of being immediately available when your tot is ready to climb out of a crib.

FEATURE CHECKLIST

When shopping for a crib, look for the following features:

☐ **Drop Sides.** Test how easily the drop side release mechanism works and how smoothly the sides raise and lower on the crib. The sides should seem sturdy and relatively easy to move. Cribs with a single drop side are *generally* more sturdy than those with double drop sides.

☐ **Hardware.** Take a look at the hooks that attach the mattress support to the crib. They should be made of solid steel rather than nylon or vinyl in order to withstand the force of a jumping tot.

☐ **Post Brackets.** The metal guide rails that support the sides as they go up and down should be sturdy metal and well attached to the crib at both the top and the bottom. Look for a nylon sleeve on the wood of the top and bottom cross rails, a feature that prevents unnecessary rattling.

☐ **Shakedown Test.** If the crib is being displayed on the showroom floor, one of the best tests is to give it a good shake to see how solid it feels.

☐ **Teething Rails.** Inspect the top of the railing on the crib sides to be sure that the plastic sheath over the wood, which is the teething rail, is firmly fastened and that the wood beneath the teething rail is finished. Inquisitive little fingers can pull the teething rails off and in some cases the underneath is brittle with sharp shards, and splintery, unfinished wood.

☐ **Wood Finishing.** Run your hand over the wooden panels and bars to see that the wood is smooth with no splinters and that the painted-on finish is even. Decorative decals on the headboard or footboard have a tendency to peel and flake off with time.

RULES FOR CRIB SAFETY

In addition to the federal mandate for the manufacture of cribs and the guidelines we suggest using when making your purchase, you should also keep the following in mind:

Avoid Plastic Bags as Mattress Liners. Dry-cleaning bags or other plastic bags should not be used to keep a crib mattress dry. The plastic can cause suffocation deaths.

Keep Hard Toys Out. Plastic toys with sharp edges or any hard toys that could be used by your tot as a foothold to get out of the crib or could be fallen on (causing eye or face injury) should be kept out of the crib.

Remove Mobiles When Outgrown. Although manufacturers put warnings on boxes about removing mobiles when a baby can sit up, parents sometimes forget. Babies can be hung on the side straps of the mobile. For the most part, the objects on mobiles such as tiny stuffed bears, or birds, or other creatures, are designed only for visual effect and not as toys to be handled directly by a baby.

Don't Use Pillows. Baby pillows, though charming, are not safe and could cause suffocation if a baby's face became buried in one. Do *not* use a baby pillow.

Position Crib Away from Window Treatment Cords. Babies have gotten caught in suspended cords when cribs are placed too near drapes or blinds with cords. This can cause strangulation. (Fasten the cords at the top of the window with a twist tie so that they remain completely out of baby's reach.)

No Jumping. Don't let your baby treat the crib like a trampoline. Babies' teeth can chip and sustain other injuries when they jump up and down in a crib and then fall into the bars or other hardware. Remove the baby from the crib when he is awake.

If Baby Can Climb Out, Change Beds. As soon as your child can get himself out of his crib, it's time to put him in a regular bed. One safe and economical alternative to immediately purchasing a bedroom suite for your toddler is to simply put the crib mattress on the floor and pack the crib away.

The following cribs are listed in alphabetical order; they are not in order of preference. You will notice that there are various kinds of cribs available to you (conventional, portable, convertible)—choose the kind that best suits your needs. But *Consumer Guide®* recommends that you shop for a crib with all of the applicable safety features that we have recommended in our "Feature Checklist."

CRIB CORNERPOST RISK

The Consumer Product Safety Commission warns that any crib cornerpost extending more than ⅝ inch above the end panel may be hazardous to your baby. These knobs can catch clothing or necklaces and cause strangulation. Manufacturers are voluntarily working towards restriction of the cornerposts to a ⅝ inch height. If you own such a crib or plan to purchase one second-hand, either unscrew the cornerposts or saw them off and sand them smooth.

COSCO CONVERTA CRIB

Model Y21   Cosco Juvenile Furniture Group Cosco Inc.

Converta Crib Model Y21 from Cosco is a small, wooden portable crib. The legs can be adjusted so that the crib sits close to the floor for use as a playpen. When in this position, it is also

safer in the event your child should fall out of it. The crib is smaller than standard size and the mattress is a 1½-inch-deep vinyl-covered foam pad. This crib is an acceptable alternative to a standard-size crib when outfitted with bumper pads.

Approximate Retail Price $75.00

MALIBU CRIB

Model 2300   Medallion Juvenile Products

Malibu Crib Model 2300 from Medallion Juvenile Products has many features to recommend it. The arched end boards give it a softer look than the traditional square shape of most cribs. The crib has only one drop side, which makes it more stable than if there were two. The drop side rail features nylon sleeves to lessen rattling, and the dual-action foot release operates easily from the center of the drop side. The rail dowels are rectangular, another feature for overall crib stability. The mattress support hooks are sturdy steel, and the mattress can be lowered to four different positions. The crib is on rollers, which simplifies cleaning the floor underneath.

Approximate Retail Price $250

NATURAL FINISH CRIB

Model 15601   Child Craft

The Natural Finish Crib from Child Craft is a simple, yet elegant crib. This model features dual drop sides that raise and lower with a lift-and-push action for maximum safety. The crib's smooth bars are an excellent safety feature and the bars go completely around the crib so that baby can see out easily, regardless of position. This full-size crib also has teething rails that adhere securely. The crib comes with easy-to-roll casters for moving and cleaning.

Approximate Retail Price   **$180**

NATURAL SORRENTO CRIB

Model 11601   Child Craft

The Natural Sorrento Crib from Child Craft is made of selected beech hardwood. This sturdy crib has a unique contemporary look to it. The crib is full size and comes equipped with steel stabilizer bars, plastic teething rails, and double drop sides that employ a stabilizer bar with toe-touch release; this requires double action on both ends to prevent accidental lowering.

Approximate Retail Price   **$225**

NIL-TO-NINETY CRIB

Model 0290   Medallion Juvenile Products

The Nil-To-Ninety crib from Medallion Juvenile Products is a versatile combination crib that features a built-in changing table at one end with convenient shelves and drawers for diaper and clothing storage. When your tot is ready to have his own bed, the crib adapts to a twin-size bed with headboard, its own nightstand, and desk. It has a genuine oak veneer. The bed uses standard crib- and twin-size mattresses. Although the initial cost is high, the combined cost of each piece of furniture would be substantially higher.

Approximate Retail Price   **$1,000**

CRADLE

OAK CRADLE
Williamsburg Collection, Connor Juvenile Furniture

The Oak Cradle from the Williamsburg Collection of Connor Juvenile Furniture has gently rounded edges, and suspends from hooks at each end of the cradle stand. A special locking pin allows you to keep the cradle motionless if you wish.

Approximate Retail Price
$145

ACCESSORIES

CARRY BED
Snugli, Inc.

The Carry Bed by Snugli is a portable bed for travel and napping. This "carry cot" has a foam padded, marshmallow vinyl mattress inside. Mesh sides give baby

a view and zip down to store flat. The bed, with nylon side bands, is available in either red and white or blue and white.

Approximate Retail Price
$50

SIMMONS DELUXE DREAMSLEEP FOAM MATTRESS

Model 9505-30   Simmons Juvenile Products Co.

The Simmons Deluxe Dreamsleep Foam Mattress is made of high-density polyurethane foam. It is a firm mattress, 5 inches high, with triple laminate vinyl covering that is made to resist cracking or tearing. The side seams are joined with heavyweight nylon binding. Four side vents permit air flow to the mattress.

Approximate Retail Price   **$55**

VISIVENT SAFETY SLEEPING SYSTEM

Century Products, Inc.

The Visivent Safety Sleeping System is a mattress *system* designed to maintain constant air flow. Baby's head rests on a removable, vented headpiece that is covered with soft netting. The headpiece is machine washable and can be removed to clean the mattress where it is most needed. The undermesh of the mattress is covered with a vinyl cover for moisture protection. The system comes with two headpieces and a fully fitted quilted crib sheet.

Approximate Retail Price   **$60**

CAR RESTRAINTS

When traveling in a passenger vehicle, your baby should *always* be correctly strapped into a car restraint—even on the first ride home from the hospital! While a car restraint is expensive (along with a crib and a stroller, this will be one of your largest shopping investments), it is absolutely necessary to use one in order to protect your child from the hazards of a car accident.

As of July 1, 1985, all 50 states have enacted legislation that requires babies and young children to be restrained in a federally approved car restraint when traveling in passenger vehicles. Most car restraint laws apply to children from birth to four years of age, with fines for noncompliance, which vary from state to state. For specific information about the law in your state (or any state into which you may be traveling), contact that state's department of transportation.

The most recent statistics available from the National Highway Traffic Safety Administration show that in 1983 more than 500 children under the age of five died as a result of passenger car accidents. An additional 31,000 children suffered injuries severe enough to require hospital treatment. In the last decade, more than 10,000 children under four years of

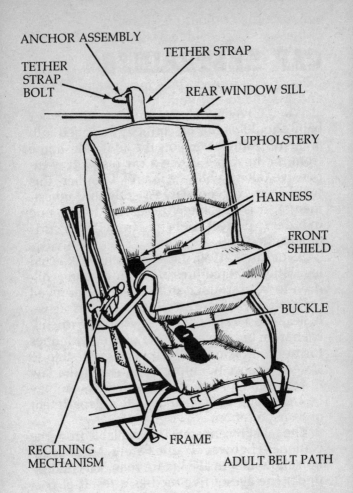

ANCHOR ASSEMBLY

TETHER STRAP

TETHER STRAP BOLT

REAR WINDOW SILL

UPHOLSTERY

HARNESS

FRONT SHIELD

BUCKLE

RECLINING MECHANISM

FRAME

ADULT BELT PATH

age have died on our highways; at least 8,000 of these children could have been saved if they had been placed in a correctly used car restraint system. (Be sure to carefully read and follow the manufacturer's instructions for use and installation of your child's car restraint; also be sure to check your automobile owner's manual for additional information and recommendations.) While it takes less than two seconds for a car accident to occur, a small, unrestrained child can thrust forward into the dashboard or into other passengers with almost 200 pounds of force.

According to federal mandate, all car restraints available in the stores must have been *dynamically tested*. This means that they have passed crash tests for cars traveling at 30 miles per hour.

Each car seat has a harness system that secures the baby to the seat with straps over each shoulder and one between the legs (this does not apply to booster seats). Once the child is placed and restrained in the car seat, facing frontward or rearward according to the car seat and size of the child, the adult seat belt is pulled over the car seat (following a specified path) and locked securely.

Since a baby's head is proportionately heavier than the rest of his body, and more vulnerable to impact and whiplash, the molded shell of the car seat (the plastic body that makes up the seat) is designed to surround the baby's head with special protection.

A close comparison of car restraints now on

the market shows very little difference in over-all quality of construction—all car restraints have sturdy harness systems and molded shells (excluding booster seats), or combination shells and steel tubing. And all car seats meet or exceed federal regulations for safety.

TETHER STRAPS

Some car seat manufacturers offer an optional tether strap that can give an additional measure of safety. The tether strap, which is attached to the top edge of the car restraint's shell and bolted to a stable spot in your car, prevents the car seat from falling forward as well as from radical side-to-side motion in the event of a car crash in excess of 30 miles per hour. Be sure to install the tether strap according to the manufacturer's instructions as well as in accordance with the information that may be available in the owner's manual for your car.

Otherwise, the safest way to install the tether strap is to have a special bolt installed in the center of your car's window sill above the back seats (a hole for the bolt must be drilled into stable metal underneath the covering of the sill). Position your child's car restraint in the center of your automobile's rear seat and adjust the tether strap so that there is no give between the car restraint and the strap. Always follow the manufacturer's directions for the correct installation of the anchor assembly and use of the car restraint and consult with your automobile owner's manual for any further instructions. The adult seat belt is still used with the tether strap. Additional anchor assemblies are available for use of the tether strap if you have more than one car in which your infant will be riding.

ADDITIONAL SAFETY TIPS

Research has shown that in the event of a car crash, your child, restrained or not, is up to 50 percent safer in the back seat than on the passenger side of the front seat where glass, bending metal, and the dashboard can cause serious injuries.

Car seats in the infant position should usually face rearward. The baby's head is supported and there is added protection of cushioning from the padded passenger seat.

Most seats require the use of the adult seat belt to secure them. Car seat manufacturers supply adapter kits if your car is equipped only with continuous-loop seat belts (a combination seat/shoulder strap where the two sections of the seat belt adjust as one unit). Car restraint harnesses should be adjusted to fit the baby snugly, and the adult seat belt should anchor the seat very firmly. **Never** use an adult seat belt alone to restrain an infant as an infant's vulnerable pelvic area can be seriously injured by the seat belt during the impact of an automobile crash.

Remember, it is primarily the harness attached to the infant car seat that protects the baby in the car seat—not the padded front railings found on some car restraint systems. Don't undermine the restraining process by neglecting to harness your baby into the car seat itself.

BOOSTER SEATS

Booster seats are an alternative product for use as a car restraint system for an older, larger child. While not as safe as a restraint with a harness, they are preferable to no car restraint at all. Booster seats are required to meet federal mandates in dynamic testing before they can be sold in the United States. But head and knee excursion (movement outward and back) distance is greater than with a regular restraint system with a harness. The advantages to a booster seat over no restraint at all are that the child is raised some three to five inches and can consequently see out the window; this helps to entertain a young passenger. Also, it trains your child to use an auto safety belt—an important habit to maintain throughout life. The booster seat will also keep the seat belt in a stationary position, something which might not happen if a child were to wriggle about in an adult seat belt. Injury could occur to a child's tender pelvic area if the seat belt were not positioned properly over your child's lap.

CAR RESTRAINTS IN AIRPLANES

The Federal Aviation Administration has recently approved the use of car seats manufactured between July 1, 1981 and February 25, 1985 for use on aircraft. These seats must bear the National Highway Traffic Safety Administration label: "This child restraint system conforms to all applicable federal motor vehicle safety standards." However, use of vest and harness-type child restraints manufactured during the same period will not be allowed on aircraft. Seats that are not so labeled and those seats manufactured before January 1, 1981, are not acceptable for use during take-off and landing. If the car restraint was manufactured after February 26, 1985, it must bear the label "This restraint is certified for use in motor vehicles and aircraft."

Despite the approval of the Federal Aviation Administration, you should still check with the specific air carrier that you are using to determine whether you will be able to carry your car seat on board the aircraft. Also, you may be required to purchase a separate ticket for the seat occupied by the child in the restraint. Call your airline in advance with any questions that you might have.

FEATURE CHECKLIST

When shopping for a car restraint, look for the following features:

- [ ] **Harness.** Check to see that latches on the harness or safety belt are easy to operate with one hand.
- [ ] **Width.** If you have a small car, you will want to look for a narrower car seat.
- [ ] **Reclining Feature.** A reclining car seat may be the best investment because it adapts to both infant and toddler sizes. It also allows babies and tots to nap comfortably while riding in the car.
- [ ] **Tethering Option.** Your baby will have additional safety at higher speeds if you purchase, install, and correctly use the tether strap that may be optional with many car seats. Rear-facing infant seats do not use tether straps. Be sure to follow the manufacturer's instructions and to check your automobile owner's manual before installing a tether strap.
- [ ] **Upholstery.** Fabric upholstery on car seats is more comfortable, but those covered in heavy vinyl are more durable and can be easily sponged clean. To test vinyl upholstery for durability, pinch it and compare the thickness of the vinyl with that of other seats. Also, check that heat welted seams are even and will not scratch baby's bare legs. The purchase of cloth covers designed for car seats will help to make baby more comfortable in warm weather.

The car restraint reviews that follow are listed in alphabetical order by product name.

While we believe that all of the car seats we recommend are "Best Buys," not every one is a best buy for you. The age, weight, and activity level of your child will affect your choice. If you have a small car or a truck, the width of the product will be more important to you. And, of course, there are budget considerations. Our purpose is that you be an educated consumer, and that the restraint you buy is the safest possible product for your baby.

CENTURY INFANT LOVE SEAT

Model 4500   Century Products, Inc.

The Century Infant Love Seat is a sturdy car seat designed for babies from birth to 20 pounds. It doubles as a portable baby carrier. As a car seat it is rearward-facing and semi-reclining to support your infant's head and critical body areas. While it is a bit on the heavy side for a baby carrier, its smooth base will protect your car upholstery as well as your furniture. A tether strap is not used with rear-facing infant safety seats.

Approximate Retail Price   **$40**

FIRST RIDE CAR SEAT CARRIER

Cosco Inc.

The Cosco First Ride Car Seat Carrier is very convenient for a baby weighing less than 20 pounds. Although reclining car seats that adapt for both infants and toddlers may be the most economical investment for long-term use, this car seat is  also economical because it is a safe car seat as well as a multi-position infant seat. Two of these positions are approved for use in a passenger car. The push-button safety harness is an excellent feature. The seat is relatively lightweight and easy to carry. The upholstery is available in padded vinyl or vinyl-backed fabric. Tether straps are not offered with rear-facing infant seats.

Approximate Retail Price **$30**

WARNING

It is not safe to carry a baby in your arms in the front seat of a car. In an accident the baby will be injured by impact with the dashboard and will receive further, more serious injury from the second impact of your body.

FISHER-PRICE CAR SEAT

Fisher-Price

The Fisher-Price Car Seat can be snapped in with one quick over-the-head motion. The release button, which is located at the base of the shield, can be unlocked with a press of the thumb for quickly installing or removing your small passenger.
The seat is deeply contoured and has self-adjusting straps. The seat adapts to either the rear-facing position for young babies or an upright "tourist" position for tots who want to be able to see out the window. The restraint secures to the adult seat with the adult seat belt threaded through slots designed for the rear-facing position and by the adult seat belt fastened through the rear tubing of the unit for the front-facing position. The padded upholstery can be easily removed and is machine washable. This car seat accommodates children from birth to 40 pounds.

Approximate Retail Price   **$65**

WARNING

Toys that fasten onto the front of children's car restraints, such as plastic steering wheels are potentially dangerous in a crash.

400 XL CAR SEAT
Models 4400 and 4446 Century Products, Inc.

The 400 XL Car Seat from Century is designed for children from birth to 43 pounds. It can be a rear- or front-facing seat. The harness and shield combination locks into place quickly and easily. The shield has two positions for use with bulky clothing. The straps on the harness are adjusted by pulling on them. It is available in vinyl or blue terry cloth.

Approximate Retail Price   **$90**

GERRY GUARDIAN CAR SEAT
Model 640 Gerico, Inc.

The Gerry Guardian Car Seat from Gerico has a self-adjusting harness that locks only on impact. That means that the harness will adapt to bulky clothing or changes in your child's size. The seat, molded of heavy-duty plastic, is designed for babies and toddlers under 40 pounds. It comes with padded seat upholstery and front chest shield. The child-proof single-touch buckle provides quick emergency release. The seat easily adjusts from a reclining to an upright position in front- and rear-facing modes.

Approximate Retail Price $70

SAFE & SOUND II

The Collier-Keyworth Company

The Collier-Keyworth Safe & Sound II, for infants from birth to 40 pounds, is a very convenient car seat to operate. This model features a three point harness system with an easy-to-use latch for quick fastening and a padded front safety shield. It can be pulled forward with one hand into a reclining position and can be used in the rear-facing position for infants. The metal parts of this system are recessed so that no hot metal parts contact the child in summer. The padded upholstery is available in poly/cotton, corduroy, or vinyl. There is no tether strap option.

Approximate Retail Price $70

STROLEE WEE CARE CAR SEAT
Model 618   Strolee
LOCKING CLIP
Model 195
TETHER STRAP
Model 205

The Strolee Wee Care Car Seat 618 features a three-position seat that adjusts from upright to deep reclining (for infants). The wide, roomy seat is especially suitable for large toddlers, particularly when they wear heavy winter coats. The upholstery is available in vinyl or in fabric, including velour and corduroy. The price will vary according to fabric choice. A spring-loaded, padded automatic shield is optional (this is not a safety feature) and can be removed easily along with the armrest. The optional Locking Clip 195 enables you to adapt continuous-loop seat belts for use with the car restraint; the optional Tether Strap 205 for the Strolee 600 series is an excellent safety feature. This seat is designed for infants from birth to 40 pounds.

Approximate Retail Price		
	Carseat	$55-75
	Locking Clip	$4
	Tether Strap	$5

40

BOOSTER CAR SEATS

CENTURY COMMANDER BOOSTER SEAT

Model 4800   Century Products, Inc.

The Century Commander Booster Seat and shield is designed to adapt to children from ages one to ten (20 to 65 pounds). The soft, padded shield is held in place by the adult seat belt, which crosses in front of it. The shield has been designed to pivot to one side for loading and unloading. Once the seat belt and shield are in place a child cannot unlock it. The seat comes in a variety of colors and fabrics and the price varies according to fabric choice. The seat has six adjustments for growth and roominess. (Note: While we do not essentially recommend booster seats, we feel that they are better than no restraint at all. See our discussion at "Booster Seats" earlier in this chapter.)

Approximate Retail Price   **$21**

VALUABLE PHONE NUMBER

The National Highway Safety Administration provides a toll-free number for you to call regarding safety defects in car restraints for children: 1-800-424-9393.

STROLEE WEE CARE BOOSTER SEAT

Model 605   Strolee

The Strolee Wee Care Booster Seat is designed for the child who has outgrown infant restraints and weighs between 20 and 70 pounds. It has a cushioned shield that adjusts as the child grows, cushioned armrests, a padded seat that comes in a variety of fabrics (the price varies according to fabric choice), and a groove for your automobile seat belt. (Note: While we do not essentially recommend booster seats, we feel that they are better than no restraint at all. See our discussion at "Booster Seats" earlier in this chapter.)

Approximate Retail Price   **$25-35**

TRAVEL HI-LO BOOSTER SEAT

Model 83A   Cosco Inc.

The Travel Hi-Lo Booster Seat from Cosco is designed for the older tot or for preschoolers; it is for use with children weighing between 20 and 65 pounds. The seat lifts the child up so that he can see out the window by either three or five inches, depending on which side of the reversible seat is used. Detachable armrests can be used in either seat position. For safest use, the restraint should be used in the rear center of the car with the tether supplied by the manufacturer bolted into metal under the rear parcel shelf of the car for maximum protection. (Note: While we do not essentially recommend booster seats, we feel that they are better than no restraint at all. See our discussion at "Booster Seats" earlier in this chapter.)

Approximate Retail Price   **$58**

TOT-RIDER QUIK-STEP BOOSTER SEAT

Model 198   Kolcraft Products, Inc.

The Kolcraft Tot-Rider Quik-Step Booster Seat is a restraint designed for the larger child (from 25 to 60 pounds) and is to be secured with your car's seat belt. It features a "Flip 'N Go" shield that allows you to place your child in the restraint quickly; the shield is padded, as are the matching armrests. The seat belt buckles around the shield, which grows with your child. This car restraint is available in five different coverings and the price varies according to the covering selected. A free locking clip for a continuous loop seat belt is included. (Note: While we do not essentially recommend booster seats, we feel that they are better than no restraint at all. See our discussion at "Booster Seats" earlier in this chapter.)

Approximate Retail Price　　　　　　　**$30**

ACCESSORIES

CARE COVERS

Bonny Bunting

Although the vinyl covers with which most car restraints are upholstered may be more durable and easier to clean, they are not especially comfortable for baby to sit on, especially in hot weather. Bonny Bunting's Care Covers have been designed for every major child car seat model (the price of the covers varies according to the model car seat you are using). They are made of soft, machine-washable fabric, with seven-layer dacron filling. The fabrics include gingham, terry cloth, and corduroy, all in a variety of colors. Care Covers are reversible and can be laced or buttoned on to the car seat. They are also available with pockets.

Approximate Retail Price　　　　　　　**$16-20**

STROLLERS AND CARRIAGES

Choosing the right stroller for your baby can make long walks around the neighborhood or trips through the shopping malls much easier. While there is a wide variety of strollers from which you can choose, not all will be right for you and your life-style. From lightweight, umbrella-handled units that fold away easily, to sturdier strollers that can handle cracked city sidewalks and curbs, American-made or imported, the choices are many.

The wisest purchase is one of the new, medium-weight models that combine both the maneuverability and collapsibility of the umbrella stroller with the postural support and durability of larger, heavier models. If you have more than one small child, investigate the double-seat strollers, but probably the most usable purchase is two lightweight umbrella strollers that can be fastened together by a latch, which can be bought separately. The least practical option is the long, heavyweight tandem stroller.

Statistics collected by the U.S. Consumer Product Safety Commission show that an estimated 42,724 babies were taken to emergency rooms for treatment of stroller-related

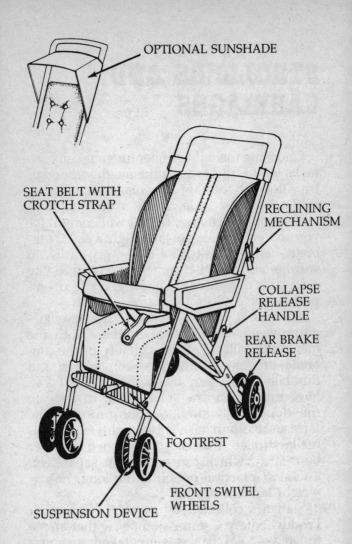

OPTIONAL SUNSHADE

SEAT BELT WITH
CROTCH STRAP

RECLINING
MECHANISM

COLLAPSE
RELEASE
HANDLE

REAR BRAKE
RELEASE

FOOTREST

FRONT SWIVEL
WHEELS

SUSPENSION DEVICE

injuries in the five years from 1980 through 1984. The major cause of injuries and even fatalities is from babies falling out of the stroller, striking their heads.

Strollers themselves present other safety hazards to babies. Babies' fingers can become entrapped or crushed in the scissoring action of the joints while the stroller is being folded. Babies have also been injured by falling into the protruding sharp edges of bolts and other metal parts. Also, many strollers, particularly the umbrella styles, are unstable and can fall over backward when a baby stands or attempts to stand up in the seat.

The Juvenile Products Manufacturers Association has established a *voluntary* safety standard for strollers and carriages. These standards were developed for JPMA by the American Society for Testing and Materials. The following is a summary of the basic safety specifications that appear in the voluntary standard:

Covered Coil Springs. There should be no exposed coil springs that could pinch or otherwise injure a child.

Brakes. The brakes should stay engaged when they are locked and should be constructed so that a child cannot release them while seated in the stroller.

Locking Device. Strollers and carriages should come equipped with a locking device that prevents accidental collapse.

Safety Belts. The stroller should come with a safety belt that is attached securely to either the stroller's frame or the upholstery. A test is to be used to assure that a baby cannot easily free herself from the belt by sliding under it or by crawling out over the top of it.

Stability. Carriages and strollers are tested on an inclined plane with weights positioned on the seating section of the stroller to see that they are stable and unlikely to tip over.

Warnings. The following warning should be permanently attached to strollers: **"Caution:** Secure child in the restraint. Never leave the child unattended." A similar warning should appear on carriages: **"Caution:** Never leave child unattended."

Unfortunately, these standards are purely voluntary; not all stroller manufacturers subject their products to these tests. Look for the JPMA label on strollers and carriages to be sure that you are purchasing one that has passed these tests. Even so, the voluntary standards for strollers and carriages fall short of what they could be. For example, there are no provisions for the quality of the restraining belt or latch on the strollers except for a series of tugs (which last less than one minute) on a babylike mannequin. While brakes are required on a unit, there are no measures to prevent accidental release by an *accompanying* child (as there are on other product safety standards). Also, there is no protection offered from the scissoring action of joints or for sharp holes in the metal tubing that could capture a child's finger, nor are there specifications for how securely caps and other protective devices must attach to the stroller's tubing and hardware. In essence, the voluntary safety standards are not a guarantee of how safe your baby will be while using one of these devices.

STROLLERS

The following are some basic rules of safety when using your stroller:

Unfold Completely. Always be sure the stroller is fully opened and in the locked position before putting baby in the stroller so that there is no danger of the device collapsing or entrapping baby's fingers.

Use the Restraint. Do not put your baby in the stroller without fastening the safety belt so that the child can't roll out, climb out, or stand up.

Handle Overload. Stroller handles weren't designed to support heavy purses, diaper bags, or shopping bags. The extra weight may allow the stroller to be more likely to fall over backward—particularly when you are unloading the baby.

Do Not Use on Stairs. Remove your baby from the stroller when ascending or descending stairs.

Look Before Crossing. Never push the baby out into the street ahead of you without first checking for on-coming traffic.

Not a Plaything. Don't allow your child to play with a stroller as if it were a toy. A child can be hurt by falling into the sharp hardware and protrusions on the stroller's frame.

Use Caution in Collapsing. Be sure that baby is completely out of range when you fold a stroller so that there is no danger of her fingers becoming entrapped.

FEATURE CHECKLIST

When shopping for a stroller, look for the following features:

☐ **Steering Ease.** Try pushing the stroller around to see how well it turns corners and how easily it maneuvers if you use only one hand. The stroller should handle well without veering to either side. A stroller with a single crossbar is easier to handle than one with umbrella-type handles.

☐ **Stability.** The stroller should be stable and unlikely to tip over when in use. If the stroller has a reclining seat, it should not be able to tip backward when baby lies down.

☐ **Collapsibility.** You should be able to fold the stroller and open it up again in one or two steps while you hold your baby. The stroller should have a locking device so that it cannot collapse accidentally.

☐ **Brakes.** Brakes should offer a positive grip on the tires so that they cannot be dislodged. The child should not be able to release the brakes while seated in the stroller.

☐ **Seat Belt.** The seat belt should actually make contact with even the smallest baby's waist. The belt material should be strong and the latches either heat welted or sewn with multiple seams. The latch should be simple for you to operate and yet require enough pressure to open so that a curious tot cannot release it inadvertently.

☐ **Shock Absorbers.** Shock absorbers are an excellent feature if you'll be walking baby along bumpy, cracked sidewalks. A stroller featuring shock absorbers will give baby a less jarring ride.

☐ **Reclining Feature.** Very young babies tend to hunch forward in a sling-type stroller seat. Tots, too, have a hard time napping in an upright position. It's useful to be able to move the stroller seat into a reclining position.

☐ **Sunshade.** Some strollers come equipped with a sunroof, although often the roof is placed so high it is only useful during the noon hour. If you plan to use the stroller in the sun, you may want to invest in a flexible-armed umbrella shade, which is offered as an option by some manufacturers.

The following strollers are listed in alphabetical order, not in order of preference. We recommend that you purchase the safest stroller that suits your life-style.

APRICA CONCOR MINI STROLLER

The Aprica Juvenile Products Division Merchants Corporation of America

The Aprica Concor Mini Stroller features dual rear brakes with shock-absorbing wheels, and a large, padded, fabric-covered seat. The stroller reclines for napping and the leg support pulls out from the seat for use in this position. A one-handed  opening and closing feature is convenient when holding baby. The stroller comes with a detachable padded guardrail, a safety belt, and a removable and adjustable sunshade.

Approximate Retail Price $100

STROLLER RECALL

In May 1983 49,000 E-Z Roller Strollers (Models 6620 and 6020) were recalled by Graco Products, Inc. The strollers, which were available between January 1982 and April 1983, could allow a baby's finger to become entrapped. Plastic hinge guard kits are available for owners. Call Graco toll free at 1-800-345-4109, or write Graco's Children's Products, P.O. Box 100, Elverson, PA 19520.

COSMOS SUPREME STROLLER

Model 971   Cosmos Trading, Inc.

The Cosmos Supreme Stroller has ballooon tires plus shock absorbers in the front and back. This gives baby a smooth ride in this sturdy but somewhat heavy stroller. The stroller's dual rear-wheel brakes lock firmly into the wheel's spokes to prevent movement. The front bar, the crossbar in back, and the seat are amply padded, as is the three-position footrest. A small button allows the option of making the wheels swivel or face straight forward. Other nice features include a sunshield hood, a rear shopping basket, and an adjustable backrest.

Approximate Retail Price   **$120**

FISHER-PRICE CARRIAGE/STROLLER

Fisher-Price

The Fisher-Price Carriage/Stroller shows care in design for baby and parent. The large back wheels and swivel front wheels make the stroller immensely maneuverable. Front-wheel shock absorbing suspension helps to soften jarring. A

cushiony, machine-washable pad covers the three-position reclining seat and two-position adjustable footrest. The stroller's pushbar adjusts to the height of the user, a comfort feature that is welcomed especially by tall parents. The stroller's rear wheels lock simultaneously when a small brake bar is pressed down with the foot. The foot-operated fold mechanism is easy to use also. The stroller has a collapsible, carriage-style hood and an under-the-seat mesh shopping shelf.

Approximate Retail Price   **$100**

GERRY HARDBACK STROLLER

Model 115   Gerico, Inc.

The Gerry Hardback Stroller is a lightweight stroller that easily folds up for storage. The back of the seat has cushioning to make baby more comfortable. The extra-wide seat accommodates a tot with a winter coat on. The seat belt latch is easy to operate, and the brakes are satisfactory. The dual swivel wheels are helpful when maneuvering.

Approximate Retail Price   **$43**

MACLAREN DOUBLE BUGGY

Model B52   Marshall Electronics, Inc.

The Maclaren Double Buggy is a double-seat stroller for families with two little ones. Each seat can be adjusted individually to an upright or a reclining position. The seats have protective side wings and supportive backs. Swivel front balloon tires make the stroller easy to handle. The brakes have triple rear action. An optional sunshade is available.

Approximate Retail Price $200

MACLAREN FULL LIE-BACK BUGGY

Model B62   Marshall Electronics, Inc.

The Maclaren Full Lie-Back Buggy has double swiveling tires on all sides for a less jarring ride for baby. The amply padded back can be stationed in three positions, including full recline for napping. The dual rear-wheel brakes lock instantly at the kick of your foot. The stroller is very easy to open and close. It comes with a removable guardrail and a safety harness. Two options are a two-piece sunshade and a clear rain cover.

Approximate Retail Price $125

OMNI CARRIAGE/STROLLER

Model 025   Evenflo Juvenile Furniture Company

The Omni Carriage/ Stroller from the Evenflo Juvenile Furniture Company (formerly Questor) has all the advantages of a baby carriage. It has protective sides and it reclines to let your baby sleep. The flip-over handle allows you to push the baby  from behind or face the baby as you push. The swivel front wheels and crossbar-style handle help make maneuvering easy. The stroller folds quickly and effortlessly. Dual positive lock brakes engage into the rear wheels, which are equipped with shock absorbers.

Approximate Retail Price   **$80**

ACCESSORIES

STROLLER PARISOL

Carriage Craft

The colorful Carriage Craft Stroller Parisol is perfect if you and your baby enjoy walking in the sun. This movable stroller parisol clamps firmly onto the tubing of any stroller. When open, it measures 28 inches across. The cotton fabric comes in a variety of colors.

Approximate Retail Price   **$15**

CARRIAGES

Baby carriages carry with them an aura of prams and nannies and walks in the park. In many European countries a baby carriage is considered a basic piece of baby equipment; mothers can be seen pushing their carriages loaded up with groceries and a toddler.

The rationale for having a baby carriage is that it allows you to take long, leisurely walks even when the baby is quite small. The carriage's high sides and hood help to protect the baby from side drafts or bright sunlight. The soothing bounce from carriage springs often helps relax babies to sleep.

But there are arguments to consider against buying a baby carriage:

Expense. New carriages usually cost well over $100, which is quite an investment in a product that will only be used for a few months.

Weight. The sheer weight of a carriage makes it awkward to use, especially if your living situation presents storage problems or if you will need to collapse it in order to carry it in the trunk of your automobile.

Awkwardness. Although a carriage may be useful for winding country roads where traffic and curbs are not problems, carriages are not very easy to maneuver on crowded city streets or over curbs.

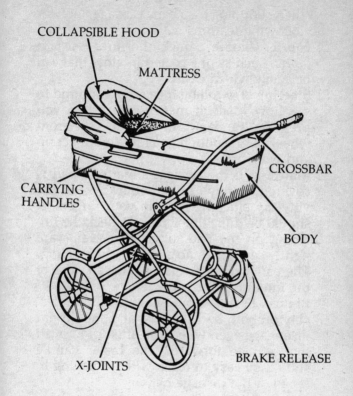

COLLAPSIBLE HOOD

MATTRESS

CROSSBAR

CARRYING
HANDLES

BODY

X-JOINTS

BRAKE RELEASE

59

FEATURE CHECKLIST

When shopping for a baby carriage, look for the following features:

☐ **Fabric.** Choose a thick, moisture-resistant fabric, such as one coated in vinyl that can be easily wiped clean.

☐ **Steering.** Try rolling the carriage around to see how easily it maneuvers. When you press on the bars, can you raise the front wheels high enough to allow you to get up and over curbs.

☐ **Mattress.** If the carriage's mattress pad is covered in vinyl, test the thickness of the vinyl by pinching it up in your fingers. It should be difficult to crease. Check the finishing on the pad to see that seams are tightly sewn with no danger of unraveling. The pad should fit flush against all sides of the interior of the carriage.

☐ **Brakes.** Brakes should hold firmly, preferably on both back wheels, and should not disengage even when you attempt to push the carriage forward. The brake handle should be easy to reach without having to let go of the carriage handle.

☐ **Interior Safety.** There should be no sharp edges from frame hardware inside the carriage bed to hurt baby's head if she's jostled during maneuvering.

☐ **Folding Ease.** The most economical unit is a two-piece carriage that doubles as a carriage and as a carry bed. Try collapsing and setting up the carriage to see how easy it is to handle. Examine the safety locks to be sure that they will prevent the carriage from folding accidentally and will hold the carry bed securely. There should be no sharp edges that could hurt your baby's fingers or your own.

☐ **Frame Safety.** Avoid carriages that have a sharp scissoring action of metal against metal at X-joints. These joints can cause crushed fingers when collapsed.

The following carriages are listed in alphabetical order and not in order of preference. When shopping for a carriage, we recommend that you purchase one with all of our recommended safety features.

CLASSICA 12 B CARRIAGE

Model 02-02-113   Perego Products Inc.

The Classica 12 B Carriage from Perego has a removable, tufted body with chrome handles that can be used as a carry bed. The detachable, lace-trimmed hood folds down and the apron has a see-through "winter-shield" for bad weather days. Inside the carriage is a supported sit-up back for baby. The folding chassis has a secure safety lock. There are chrome fenders over the white, 12-inch balloon tires, and all four wheels have brakes that work in conjunction with two non-tip stands.

Approximate Retail Price   **$200**

MACLAREN EUROPA PRAM BUGGY
Model X0397 and X040   **Marshall Electronics, Inc.**

The Maclaren Europa Pram Buggy from Marshall Electronics has multiple uses as a carriage, a portable hooded bed, and a stroller. The carriage's chassis folds down quickly so that it can be toted by its umbrella handles with one hand while the baby bed section can be carried with the other, which is useful for stairs, riding buses, or storage. The frame has four double-balloon tires that swivel in the front when it is converted into a baby stroller. The stroller's seat can be reclined into a semi-upright position. It has dual rear brakes. The washable fabric material is available in burgundy or blue. Optional accessories are a sunshade and a rain cover for added protection for your baby.

Approximate Retail Price   **$250**

SILVER CROSS "MALMO" CARRIAGE

Carriage Craft, Inc.

Silver Cross carriages can be considered the top-of-the-line product in the carriage world. They feature carriages that cost more than $600. The Malmo is the least expensive of their carriages. It has a soft, fabric-covered body that can be detached from the hardware and carried separately. The 10½-inch wheels are removable. Other features are a fitted storm flap and chrome carrying handles on the bed. It has a fully lined hood that adjusts to a half-way position to block drafts.

Approximate Retail Price   **$240**

HIGH CHAIRS

While a high chair is not something you will need to have in your home the moment baby arrives from the hospital, it is a large enough investment that you will want to spend time carefully considering the features and options you prefer before you make a purchase.

A high chair is helpful to you because it positions your baby at a comfortable level during baby's mealtimes. Unfortunately, a high chair's long legs, instability, and loosely fitting tray make them less than safe. According to the National Injury Information Clearing House of the Consumer Product Safety Commission, over 46,000 babies or their parents required trips to emergency rooms for injuries resulting from high chairs in the years between 1979 and 1984.

Major injuries to babies occur when they fall out of their high chair, or fall over *with* their chairs after having stood up. In some cases the trays have given way so that babies fall on top of them. Babies also can cut their fingers on sharp-edged hardware designed to hold the tray onto the high chair. A typical adult injury results from toes stubbed on the high chair legs.

Like strollers and playpens, high chairs are only governed by a *voluntary* safety standard

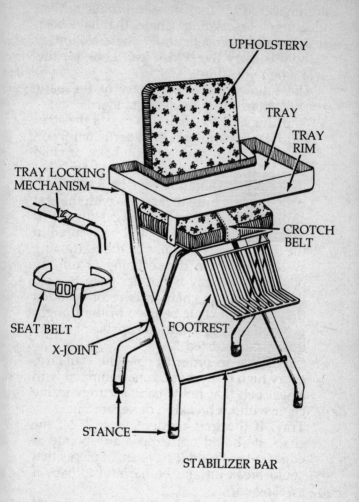

UPHOLSTERY

TRAY

TRAY RIM

TRAY LOCKING MECHANISM

CROTCH BELT

SEAT BELT

X-JOINT

FOOTREST

STANCE

STABILIZER BAR

administered by the Juvenile Products Manufacturers Association. Chairs that have been tested and approved under these voluntary standards carry the JPMA seal. Look for this seal when you shop.

The following is a summary of the basic specifications for high chair standards:

Warnings. Every chair that passes the standard has a warning posted permanently on the high chair stating that a baby or child should never be left unattended and that the seat belt should always be used. Similarly, the brochure that comes with the seat should have the following statement: **"Warning.** The child should be secured in the high chair at all times by the restraining system, either in the reclining or upright position. The tray is not designed to hold the child in the chair. It is recommended that the high chair be used in the upright position only by children capable of sitting upright unassisted."

Seat Belts. In order to pass the standard, every high chair must come equipped with a seat belt that holds baby securely in the chair without breaking or separating.

Tray. If the tray accidentally falls off the chair, it should not expose any points or edges, nor should it have small pieces that could break off and be harmful to baby if swallowed.

Tray Fastening Strength. The tray should stay put when locked on as demonstrated by pull tests from a number of positions.

Latch Springs on Tray. If the tray latches with wide coils, they should be covered so that small fingers could not conceivably be caught in them.

Surfaces. The surfaces are to be easy to clean with a finish that won't peel or bubble and with no edges, protrusions, or points that could hurt a baby who fell on them.

Locking Mechanism. High chairs that fold must have a locking device or be designed so that they can't fold or collapse accidentally.

Caps. The covers that protect sharp edges, points, or protruding hardware should be difficult to remove so that a baby can't take them off.

Stability. The chair should be hard to tip over.

Folding Safety. There should be no danger of a baby's fingers being crushed as metal bars collapse on each other in a scissoring action.

Footrest and Seat Strength. The footrest and seat should be able to support heavy weight without breaking or bending.

Wood. Wood must be free from splinters.

These specifications are from the Standard Consumer Safety Specifications for High Chairs, formulated by the American Society for Testing and Materials and used by the JPMA.

FEATURE CHECKLIST

When shopping for a high chair, look for the following features:

☐ **Tray Removal.** Test the tray to see if it can be easily removed with one hand. Look for a tray with multiple positions that will fit close in when baby is small and then move out to a wider position as baby grows.

☐ **Tray Rim.** A deep, wraparound tray made of sturdy, washable plastic with a raised edge that holds liquid spills is a good feature.

☐ **Cleaning Ease.** Look for a high chair that can be quickly wiped clean after meals; be sure there are no small nooks or crannies that can harbor dried food. Vinyl and plastic upholstery are easiest to sponge clean.

☐ **Safety Belt.** Since falling from high chairs is a major cause of baby injuries in the kitchen, don't trust the high chair tray to restrain your baby. Look for a seat belt that is sturdy and has a latch that can open easily with one hand but needs enough pressure that a child will be unable to open it.

☐ **Ease of Collapsing.** Most parents will have their baby's high chair up for the two or more years that their baby uses it, but it is nice to be able to pack a chair away when you need more space or when you want to take the chair with you on a trip. Be sure, though, that the high chair cannot collapse while baby is sitting in it.

The high chairs that follow are listed in alphabetical order rather than in order of preference. The high chair that might be a "Best Buy" for you may not be for another consumer. *Consumer Guide®* suggests that you look for all of the safety features that we recommend in our "Feature Checklist."

FISHER-PRICE HIGH CHAIR

Fisher-Price

The Fisher-Price High Chair features a large wraparound tray that can be removed with one hand when you depress a tab on either side of the tray. The tray has a deep, spill-catching rim; raised elbow rests; and a sloping tray surface that help keep

baby clean. A tab in front allows you to slide the tray back and forth with one hand. The well-padded vinyl seat cushion can be completely removed for quick and easy clean up. It has a quick snap-lock seat belt for safety. There's an adjustable footrest (three positions), and the chair folds down easily for storage. This high chair is made of chrome and plastic.

Approximate Retail Price   **$63**

KANTWET SIDEWINDER HIGH CHAIR

Kantwet Division of Evenflo Juvenile Furniture Company

The Kantwet Sidewinder High Chair from Evenflo (formerly Questor) is a chrome-plated steel high chair. Its main attraction is its tray. With a one-handed release mechanism you can swing the tray down to hang at one side, or, if you wish, you can slide this high-edged, sturdy plastic tray completely off the chair's armrest. The tray will also stay in the (straight up) open position by itself, freeing your hands for baby. The padded vinyl seat and seat back are completely washable, and the chair has a three-position footrest. The high chair comes with a sturdy safety strap. It folds flat and can convert easily to a youth chair or a utility chair.

Approximate Retail Price   **$50**

PRIDE-TRIMBLE HIGH CHAIR

Model 237   Pride-Trimble Corporation

The Pride-Trimble High Chair Model 237 has a jumbo-sized plastic tray with a deep rim that slides to three positions. It also has an optional swing-away tray feature with one hand operation. All of this adjusts with a single side button. The 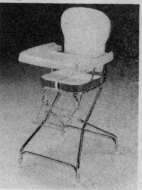 chrome steel frame has front and rear stabilizing bars. The chair's wide stance has been designed to prevent accidental folding while a baby is sitting in it. There's a convenient towel rack on the back of the chair. It has an adjustable restraining strap with a two-sided release. The wide, amply padded backrest and seat are available in a variety of colors and in fabric or vinyl upholstery. The arms can be folded away to convert the high chair into a youth chair or a utility chair for adults.

Approximate Retail Price   **$55**

STROLEE PLUSH HIGH CHAIR

Model 414 Strolee

The Strolee Plush High Chair Model 414 has a unique gravity-centered design that makes it impossible to fold when a baby is seated in it. When the baby's out of the chair, it can be folded with a one-handed action. The large, plastic wraparound  tray has a deep rim to prevent spills from reaching the floor. The tray can be released and inserted on the chair with a single push-button maneuver. The chrome and vinyl high chair has a wide sculptured back with button tufting, and is available in corduroy and velour in a variety of colors (the price varies according to fabric). The footrest adjusts to four positions. The chair has been designed to be table height and the side arms can easily be folded away to make the chair usable by older children and adults. The seat belt features a squeeze-release buckle.

Approximate Retail Price   **$60–70**

BOOSTER SEATS

FISHER-PRICE BOOSTER SEAT
Fisher-Price

The Fisher-Price Booster Seat is a bright, colorful seat with Sesame Street graphics of the Muppet characters on a yellow school bus or of a fire truck. Climbing aboard makes mealtime fun for tots. The snap-lock safety belt attaches to an  adult-size chair to prevent tipping. The seat can also be used on the floor (without the safety belt) for watching TV or other activities. The high, side walls of the seat help contain the child and large nonskid feet hold the seat in place. The seat's smooth surface means easy cleaning of spills and crumbs.

Approximate Retail Price   **$10**

INFANSEAT 4 STAGE BOOSTER SEAT

Model 260   Evenflo Juvenile Furniture Company

The Infanseat 4 Stage Booster Seat from Evenflo (formerly Questor) is made of sturdy, lightweight molded plastic. It offers four different seating levels according to your child's needs. A 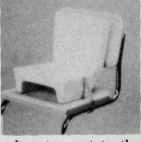 safety strap secures the booster seat to the chair. Nonskid pads on the base help to make the seat even safer. The booster folds to make a case with carrying handle for easy travel.

Approximate Retail Price   **$15**

FOLDING SASSY REPAIR

Models 021 and 023 Folding Sassy Seats are involved in a voluntary repair program due to stress cracks that have developed around the restraint horn and locking pin tabs. This does not affect the Original or Deluxe Sassy Seat. The chairs can be identified by the use of round aluminum tubing on the chair. Consumers should send their name, address, phone number and store of purchase to Sassy Inc., 191 Waukegan Rd., Northfield, IL 60093. Retailers have been notified and have received replacement parts.

PLAYPENS

Playpens (euphemistically called "play yards" by manufacturers) are framed enclosures designed to temporarily confine a baby. They are meant to be used by babies that weigh under 30 pounds and are less than 34 inches in height, according to the Juvenile Products Manufacturers Association.

Until you are certain that you need a playpen to restrain your baby, we suggest that you purchase your other major baby equipment first (crib, car seat, high chair, stroller) and buy a playpen only if you decide you will use one.

The value of a playpen is that it offers a secure place for your baby while you're busy with household chores. A playpen can be a safety device when you're cooking in the kitchen and your baby or toddler might otherwise be underfoot.

The disadvantage of a playpen is that it may frustrate the strong exploratory drives of your baby—a naturally curious being—who wants to see, touch, and experience the world without being restrained.

On a day-to-day basis, parents only find a playpen useful for very short periods of time. And many babies actively resist being cooped up and separated from the rest of their family. For most households the playpen eventually

A DANGEROUS MESH PLAYPEN

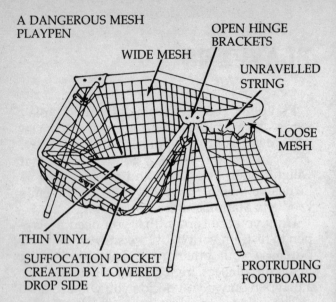

WIDE MESH

OPEN HINGE BRACKETS

UNRAVELLED STRING

LOOSE MESH

THIN VINYL

SUFFOCATION POCKET CREATED BY LOWERED DROP SIDE

PROTRUDING FOOTBOARD

SAFE MESH PLAYPEN

COVERED HARDWARE

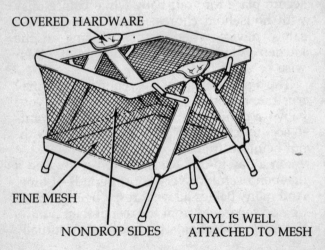

FINE MESH

NONDROP SIDES

VINYL IS WELL ATTACHED TO MESH

becomes a bulky, and possibly unsafe, toy depository that takes up needed space in the living room or nursery.

There are two basic types of playpens: those constructed of wood and those made with metal tubing and nylon mesh. Wooden playpens are usually heavier than mesh-sided pens; they fold down when their two hinged sides sandwich inward as the two floor panels lift up from the center. Mesh-sided playpens, on the other hand, call for a variety of folding maneuvers, in some cases even requiring that the playpen be turned completely upside down.

Mesh-sided playpens come in a variety of sizes and shapes from rectangular crib-sized models to larger square and multi-paneled designs. The supportive tubing of the playpen is usually constructed of chrome, chrome-plated metal, or aluminum. Some models have straight legs with caps to protect floor surfaces, while others have a bent-tube design so that uncovered metal U-joints may contact the floor—a possible disadvantage for abrasion and rust stains.

Most soft-sided playpens use vinyl with heat-welted seams for a border at the base of the mesh (providing draft protection) and at the top of the playpen to cover the hinge assembly and the bars. More expensive models have thick foam padding between the vinyl and the bars to prevent injuries to babies should they fall.

SAFETY PROBLEMS

Playpen injuries serious enough to send babies to hospital emergency rooms tripled between 1980 and 1983 in the United States. In 1984, 3,220 babies were involved in playpen-related accidents. According to estimates of the U.S. Consumer Product Safety Commission, nearly 12,000 babies were injured in playpen accidents between 1980 and 1984.

PLAY IT SAFE WITH MESH PLAYPENS

The potentially fatal suffocation pocket currently existing in mesh-sided playpens (with a side in the down position) and the possibility of strangulation suggest that you should use caution in putting your baby into one. If you *do* purchase a mesh-sided playpen, we advise using the following precautions:

Supervise Your Baby. You should never leave your baby alone to play in a playpen without being able to see and hear him.

Keep Sides Up. Rather than using the drop-side feature on a mesh-sided playpen, with the danger of suffocation and finger injury, we suggest that you leave the sides up permanently when the playpen is in use.

Look for Loose Threads. Curious fingers can find loose threads that join the mesh to the vinyl trim. A pulled thread can create dangerous gaps in the playpen as well as tangle around baby, cutting off circulation. It can also get into a baby's mouth.

Avoid Using a Playpen with Torn Sides. If the mesh develops holes, *do not continue to use the playpen.* Babies can strangle or get caught; even the smallest hole presents a possible danger.

Teething. Do not permit your baby to chew on the mesh or vinyl parts of the playpen. Teeth can become caught and damaged as a result.

Open and Close Carefully. Don't allow the baby to be near the playpen when you open it or collapse it. Place your baby securely in an infant seat or high chair until you have the playpen ready for storage or use.

Fasten the Padding Down. So that there is no danger of your baby falling onto the hard floor or getting hurt when the padding shifts, we suggest fastening the pad down by sewing two fabric strips onto each side of the pad; the strips should be long enough to be tied across the underside of the playpen in order to hold the pad securely in place.

VOLUNTARY STANDARDS

Fortunately, the Juvenile Products Manufacturers Association has established voluntary safety standards that eliminates many of the safety problems of mesh and hinges. Because the safety standards are voluntary and not mandatory, manufacturers are not required to follow them. Those manufacturers who do comply with the voluntary standards have their playpens tested by an independent testing laboratory to assure that the playpens pass the standards. If a playpen passes the standards, the JPMA seal will be displayed on the product's packaging or on the product.

The following is a summary of the main points of the JPMA voluntary safety standards:

Wooden Playpens. Wooden playpens must be finished so that they are free of splinters and have bars no wider than 2⅜ inches apart so that a baby's body cannot slip through, leaving the head entrapped, causing strangulation.

Railing Strength. The railings of the playpen must be strong enough to withstand a baby's weight without breaking, falling, or bending.

Mesh Sides. The weave of the mesh should be designed to prevent a baby's fingers, toes, or buttons on clothing from getting caught.

Locking Devices. The playpen should come equipped with a locking device to prevent it from accidentally folding up or being lowered by the baby. Operating the lock must take more strength than a baby possesses. The unlocking of the playpen's sides is required to take more than one action to prevent a baby from being able to do it.

Upholstery. Thick vinyl upholstery should be used to prevent the baby from chewing off pieces and swallowing it.

Floors. The bottom floor of a playpen should be strong enough to withstand both a heavy weight and the type of stresses caused by a jumping baby (measured during testing by a repetitive drop of a 30 pound weight).

Sharp Edges. There should be no sharp edges, protrusions, or points that could hurt a baby who fell into them.

Height. To prevent a baby from climbing out, side railings must be at least 20 inches tall.

Pinch Potential. Playpens should be constructed with minimal potential for scissoring, shearing, or pinching injuries.

Warning. The following warning must appear on all mesh-sided playpens: "**Warning.** Never leave infant in play yard with sides down. Infant may roll into space between pad and loose mesh side causing suffocation."

The specifications for playpens were formulated by the American Society for Testing and Materials for the JPMA. It's wise to shop for a playpen that passes the Juvenile Products Manufacturers Association safety specifications.

WOODEN PLAYPENS

Given the incidence of injury to babies in mesh-sided playpens, you may decide to purchase a wooden playpen. Beyond safety considerations, the clear advantages to a wooden playpen are that it offers a less restricted view of the outside world than mesh and the wooden spindles can serve as a support to a baby when sitting or pulling to a stand.

But there are shortcomings to wooden playpens. They are heavy and awkward to move, and the hard bars may cause bruising if a baby falls into them. Yet, even considering these limitations, the wooden playpen is still the safest buy until more manufacturers come to grips with the suffocation problem of mesh-sided playpens. (Some manufacturers have; see the reviews that follow.)

FEATURE CHECKLIST

When shopping for a playpen, look for the following features:

☐ **Hinges.** From a baby's height examine the action of the hardware where the playpen's sides fold and fasten. Be sure there is not a clamping or scissoring action that might entrap or cut your baby's fingers.

☐ **Tube Joints.** If the tubes in a mesh-sided playpen open and close with a scissoring action, examine the contact point to see that the manufacturer has built in a buffer space between the two tubes so that a baby's fingers cannot be trapped.

- ☐ **Mesh.** If a mesh-sided playpen is your only option, choose a model with finely woven mesh according to the Juvenile Products Manufacturers Association voluntary standards listed above. Some older playpens have a wide mesh that make them less safe.

- ☐ **Vinyl Padding.** Compare the padding of several different models by pinching the vinyl between your fingers. Thick vinyl is difficult to crease and has a heavy feel to it when it is separated from the padding. Thin vinyl pinches up and creases easily, and it is less durable and more likely to tear.

- ☐ **Seams.** Most vinyl seams are either heat welted, which leaves a sharp rim where the two edges of vinyl have been melted together, or they are machine stitched. Look for seams that are smooth to the touch. Heat-welted seam lines should appear even to ensure that there is no problem with splitting. Machine-stitched seams should leave no dangling threads, gaps, or holes where the seam has missed the vinyl.

- ☐ **Floor.** Look at how the floor of the playpen is finished. Be sure there are no metal staples or hardware that might conceivably be pulled loose by your baby and swallowed. Look to see that there are no sharp bolt heads that your baby might fall on if the padding slips out of place. Try pressing on the floorboard in order to test its strength. Select a floor that holds steady without bending to your pressure; active, jumping

babies may cause a thin floorboard to crack.
- ☐ **Teething Rails.** On wooden playpens look for teething rails on all four sides of the unit. The teething rails should adhere securely so that curious fingers cannot get under them.

The following playpens are listed in alphabetical order and not in order of preference. When shopping for a playpen, be sure to look for all of the safety features listed in our "Feature Checklist."

HEDSTROM PLAY YARD (WOODEN)

Models 6–543 and 6–941   Hedstrom

The Hedstrom Play Yard has a sturdy floor and smooth finish. The teething rails on the sides of the playpen stay firmly in place in spite of small, curious fingers. It has turned corner posts for safety and casters that make rolling easy. There are several bar designs available, but we recommend the smooth, simple pole finish for safety and ease of cleaning.

Approximate Retail Price   **$75**

NORTH STATES WOODEN PLAY YARD

Models 3552 and 3553
North States Industries, Inc.

The Play Yard by North States is a wooden playpen featuring smoothly finished hardwood bars with teething rails on the top of all crossbars. There are double locking hinges on  the sides and plastic casters for moving the playpen. The floor is constructed of tempered hardboard and it comes with a vinyl-covered foam pad. The play yard is available in natural or walnut finish.

Approximate Retail Price $70

NU-LINE KIDDIE YARD

Model 5117   Nu-Line Industries
The Kiddie Yard by Nu-Line is a *hard* plastic-mesh play yard designed for use out-of-doors. This large wooden play yard opens up to 17 square feet. It comes with four ground stakes to 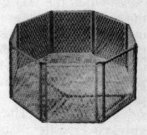 hold it in place and we strongly recommend

that you *not* use the play yard without these stakes. Because there are eight panels to the unit, it does not necessarily have to remain in the traditional square; it can conform to a variety of shapes. Each panel is made of hard plastic mesh within a weather-resistant hardwood frame. It folds easily and comes with a carrying strap for portability.

Approximate Retail Price   **$35**

WELSH PLAY PEN

Model 4275 Welsh Company

The Play Pen by the Welsh Company is the first one designed to address the safety issue of the "suffocation pocket" in mesh-sided playpens. This mesh-sided playpen has no drop sides, so it cannot be used with the sides down. For collapsing, both sides fold down simultaneously when the floorboard is folded up from the center. The legs are made of three-quarter-inch chrome-plated steel and all potential pinch points or finger hazards have been eliminated. The playpen's feet have plastic caps to protect your floor. A thick vinyl is used for the padded top railing, padded hinge covers, and sidebar cushions. The playpen comes with a vinyl-covered floor cushion.

Approximate Retail Price   **$70**

INFANT CARRIERS AND SWINGS

Infant carriers and swings may be called luxury items because you *can* manage without them. Infant carriers are a bit more functional than swings because they allow you to prop baby up to watch you as you work around the house and you can use them to hold your baby while you feed her. But even so, they are limited in the length of time you can use them. Once baby is able to sit up on her own and crawl around, she detests being strapped down. Swings are also limited in the length of time you will use them, but they often help calm a fretful baby.

INFANT CARRIERS

Safety statistics show that approximately 5,000 babies have been injured seriously enough to need emergency room treatment in infant carrier-related accidents over the past four years. The most serious accidents occur when the infant carriers fall off tables, counters, or other high places, when the seat's frame collapses, or when baby's own movements have caused the carrier to fall.

Serious injury has also occurred when an adult who is carrying a baby in an infant carrier trips and falls, throwing their small passenger to the ground. Care should be taken when carrying your child in an infant carrier so that you can always see your path. Also, do not use the stand of the carrier as a handle unless expressly designed for that purpose. Read the packaging carefully.

Unless otherwise stated by the manufacturer, infant carriers are absolutely *not* to be substituted for a car restraining system. Some car safety seats are designed for use as both, but most infant carriers do not meet any of the necessary requirements for use as a car restraint.

FEATURE CHECKLIST

When shopping for an infant carrier, look for the following features:

☐ **Stability.** Test the carrier with your arm and elbow to see if it is sturdy enough to stay upright when weight shifts from one side to another.

☐ **Nonslip Feet.** The base of the carrier should always have a nonslip surface to prevent baby's motions from "walking" it off the edge of shiny tables or other smooth surfaces.

☐ **Seat Belt.** The carrier should come with a safety belt. Examine the belt to see that the latch is securely fastened to the belt and that it is easy to operate, holds firmly without slipping, and can adjust with ease.

☐ **Adjustable Positions.** A good infant carrier should offer several different positions from reclining to upright.

☐ **Cleaning Ease.** Choose a carrier upholstered in vinyl or other water-resistant material to make spills and crumbs easy to clean up.

The infant carrier reviews that follow are listed in alphabetical order by product name. While we believe that all of the infant carriers that we recommend are "Best Buys," not every one is a best buy for you. Review our checklist and choose a product that meets those recommendations that deal with safety.

CRADLEMATE BABY CARRIER

Model 550   Cosco Inc.

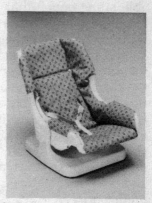

The Cradlemate Baby Carrier by Cosco is an adjustable carrier that allows you to put baby in one of three positions with the push of side-locking buttons. The large, molded pedestal base with a nonskid surface provides excellent stability. There's a safety belt to secure baby and a handhold that permits easy carrying. The design of the base allows you to place the carrier on chairs, and the roomy shell is covered with a fully padded vinyl seat. This is not designed as a car restraint and should not be used as such.

Approximate Retail Price   **$20**

KANGA-ROCKA-ROO ROCKING CARRIER

Model 1551   Century Products, Inc.

The Kanga-Rocka-Roo Rocking Carrier from Century Products has a convenient, multi-position handle that adjusts for carrying, reclining, rocking, and storage. Push buttons lock the handle quickly into position. The carrier has a removable fabric pouch that holds baby items such as diapers and bottles, or it can hold *your* things. The sturdy shell is molded plastic with a vinyl-padded cushion and nonskid grippers for safety. A stabilizer bar on the bottom of the carrier allows the built-in rocker to sit upright. Its larger size accommodates heavy clothing and the woven T-strap safety belt has a quick-lock buckle. The Kanga-Rocka-Roo has such options as a soft, washable fabric cover; a sheepskinlike cover; a molded plastic pouch; and a music feature, each for a somewhat higher price.

Approximate Retail Price   **$24**

EXERCISER SEAT

GERRY BABY SEAT

Model 305   Gerico, Inc.

The Gerry Baby Seat is an American version of a jumper seat that has been popular in Europe for babies up to 12 months of age. The seat has a gentle, bouncing action created by the baby's motions. It also has a crotch and waist belt that is necessary for safety with this type of seat. The wide-based chrome steel frame of the seat has small washers to lessen sliding. The seat is upholstered in fully washable cotton-blend fabric. Its reclining position is convenient for napping, and a footrest adds support for small infants. This is not recommended for use on tables or other high surfaces.

Approximate Retail Price   **$23.50**

SWINGS

Parents often feel that automatic baby swings are helpful since a repetitive tick-tock sound lulls a baby into contentedness. The disadvantage of a baby swing is that it takes up a lot of space, and for the price is only useful for a short period of time.

Swings are not a substitute for parent-baby contact, so it's wise to limit swing use to those brief periods of the day when you need a break and the baby seems to respond to the lulling motions of the swing.

A word of caution is in order. Be sure that you always use the seat belt on the swing seat. Young babies can fall forward into the vinyl-padded bar of an older model swing causing near suffocation. Older babies have toppled out or caused the swing to collapse. As with other baby equipment, do not leave your child unattended in a baby swing.

We firmly do *not* recommend the Gerry Bear 3 Baby Swing because in our opinion there is a potential strangulation hazard posed by the swing's activating mechanism. This mechanism is a plastic bear that slowly moves up one side of a leg of the swing, using a flexible cord that can be pulled out from the swing leg. The cord could conceivably entrap the neck of a baby or toddler who is playing outside of the swing. Hundreds of deaths have been caused by drapery and blind cords and we feel that the same entanglement hazard might exist in this product.

FEATURE CHECKLIST

When shopping for a baby swing, look for the following features:

□ **Safety Belts.** Safety belts should be easy-to-use, sturdy, adjustable, and able to hold firmly. Use them every time you put your baby in the swing.

□ **Running Time.** If you have a choice between different models, choose the one with the longest running time. Otherwise, you'll find that baby barely dozes off before being awakened when the swing stops moving.

□ **Stability and Sturdiness.** Check the stance of the swing to see if it feels sturdy when you shake it. Try to tip it over to see how well the legs hold.

□ **Storage Ease.** Swings take up a great deal of floor space. See how easily the swing can be stored and whether it will fit into the space you have available.

□ **Seat Positions.** A dual position seat that both reclines and sits more upright will be useful for baby when she's small or when she dozes off.

The baby swings in the following reviews are listed in alphabetical order by brand name. We have not listed them by preference. When shopping for a swing, be sure to look for all of the safety features that are listed in our "Feature Checklist."

NON-STOP SWYNGOMATIC

Model 14401   Graco Children's Products, Inc.

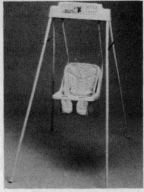

The Non-Stop Swyn-
gomatic from Graco
runs for up to 150
hours on two D-cell
batteries. The quiet
rocking motion of the
swing has a soothing
effect on baby, and
because there isn't a
noisy wind-up device
(that needs to be re-
wound at short inter-
vals) your infant won't be startled out of a nap.
It has a stable, easy-access frame and the reclining seat is nicely designed with two reclining positions. The seat belt is wide and sturdy.
The legs of the unit can be folded together for
temporary storage and by removing a few
screws it can be put away for long-term storage. This model also comes with a music option for a somewhat higher price.

Approximate Retail Price $60

SUPERTRONIC SWING

Model 12-423   Century Products, Inc.

Century's Super-tronic Swing is a stable swing that provides up to 100 hours of effortless swing time for your infant on four flashlight batteries. The quieter operation won't startle your baby and it has an easy shut-off mechanism to save on battery power. The molded plastic seat, which stops swinging when you hold on to it, comes with a fabric or vinyl cushion and has two reclining positions. The wide seat belt is adjustable. The swing does not fold up for storage.

Approximate Retail Price   **$60**

SWYNGOMATIC SWING/INFANT CARRIER

Model 7600   Graco Children's Products, Inc.

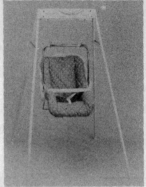

The Swyngomatic Swing/Infant Carrier by Graco has a nicely designed seat that simply hooks over the swinging mechanism so that it can be removed to serve as an all-purpose infant carrier around the house. The carrier has a soft washable fabric seat cover, a crotch strap to keep baby from slipping out, and a latching safety belt for added security. The carrier's nonslip foot pads help to keep it from slipping when it's removed and used as an infant seat on smooth surfaces. The carrier reclines for sleeping or very small babies. The swing mechanism operates quietly for 15 minutes per windup. The legs fold together for storage.

Approximate Retail Price   **$45**

INFANT "POUCH" CARRIERS AND FRAME CARRIERS

Infant "pouch" carriers and tubular-framed back pack carriers are a popular way to carry a baby. Soft carriers are especially useful for the newborn and young baby who will usually be soothed by the involvement with your body's rhythmic movement. Some carriers are designed to have baby facing outward, away from your body. But most carriers snuggle your baby close to your chest, which is a preferable arrangement for the very young baby. Fabric carriers can often be used by the older, heavier baby, but because they don't offer the additional support of a frame, they tend to make a larger baby feel like a heavy burden on your shoulders.

Fabric carriers have been found to be especially effective in soothing fussy babies. It may be that the body-to-body closeness provided by the pack and its motions are exactly what a fussy baby needs to provide an extra sense of security. If your baby is soothed by the pack, consider wearing it indoors while you do household chores.

Tubular-framed back packs are only designed for use on your back. They are made especially for the baby over six months of age who can sit up and who loves viewing the world from over your shoulders. The frame of the carrier helps to redistribute some of your baby's weight off your shoulders and onto your back. Frame packs don't make the baby any lighter than she really is, though, so it's wise to gradually break your body in by building up your carrying time slowly.

The point at which your baby's weight begins to stress your body is when she reaches approximately one fourth of your own body weight. As your baby passes that proportion of your weight, you are more likely to injure your back in lifting her and feel fatigue when carrying her for long periods of time. Brisk walking with a baby in a frame carrier is far more comfortable than passive activities that require standing still with the pack on.

FEATURE CHECKLIST

When shopping for a soft carrier, look for the following features:

☐ **Fabric Strength.** The fabric of the carrier should be heavyweight. Corduroy, cotton/polyester, and denim are excellent choices.

☐ **Seams.** Check the seams to see that they are well finished, especially at points of stress such as where the straps are fastened to the pack.

☐ **Washability.** The carrier should be completely machine washable.

□ **Ease of Putting On.** Most fabric carriers seem like a maze of straps and clanking hardware when you initially take them out of the package. The best test of how easy the pack will be to use is to actually try it on following the manufacturer's directions.

□ **Shoulder Padding.** Firm, thick shoulder padding is a must for maximum parental comfort.

□ **Fit.** Try the pack on for size. If you are short or small framed, some carriers may be too long to fit you correctly, or their shoulder straps may be positioned too far apart to stay on your shoulders well.

□ **Strap Fastenings.** The fasteners that attach the pack's straps to the carrier should be heavy duty, preferably made of metal. Fastenings should be easy to adjust and able to hold baby's weight securely.

□ **Crotch Width.** The seat should not force the baby's legs into an uncomfortable splayed position.

□ **Leg Holes.** The holes for baby's legs should not be higher than the seat, or they may restrict the circulation in your baby's legs. The leg holes themselves should be soft and not scratchy for maximum comfort.

□ **Adjustments.** The pack should accommodate different sizes and weights of babies from very tiny ones who need head and upper body support to toddlers who need more body freedom. Read the manufacturer's instructions on how to adapt the pack to the older baby or young child.

- ☐ **Head Support.** Young babies need head support. Look for built-in head support in the way the outer pack fits around the baby's head or for special flexible mesh supports that prevent baby's head from flopping.
- ☐ **Nursing Option.** If you plan to nurse, you may want a carrier with a discreet zipper for nursing so that you won't have to take your baby out of the carrier. If there isn't a nursing zipper, read the manufacturer's instructions on how the carrier may be used while breastfeeding.

GERRY CUDDLEPACK

Models 080, 075—48 and 075—55   Gerico, Inc.

Gerry Cuddlepacks are designed to be used on either your chest or your back. An adjustable headrest gives padded head and neck support to the small baby. The inner seat adjusts with an easy-to-use drawstring. Well-padded shoulder straps and the adjustable waist strap with one-hand release buckle make the carriers a superior product. Each carrier comes with a removable soft bib, and both carrier and bib are fully washable. An interior zipper enables baby to nurse while still in the pack. The model

080 features a removable, insulated quilted liner for cold weather. Model 075-55 is a lightweight cotton carrier with a breathable mesh lining for hot weather use. Model 075-48 in navy corduroy is more suitable for moderate temperatures.

Approximate Retail Price $35

SNUGLI CARRIER

Snugli, Inc.

The Snugli consists of a fabric dual-pouch system: the inner pouch seat holds the baby and the outer pouch, with its tucked neck collar, gives support to the head. The inner pouch is adjustable to three positions for babies from birth to six months. As your baby grows, the seams can be let out to enlarge the carrier. The Snugli, which can be worn either on the chest or on the back, has amply padded shoulder straps, and secure, easy-to-operate buckles. A sash at the lower end of the carrier ties around the adult's waist for extra support. Constructed with brightly colored corduroys or lightweight seersucker, Snuglis are also available in a less expensive denim model.

Approximate Retail Price $40

FRAME CARRIER

FEATURE CHECKLIST

When shopping for a frame carrier, look for the following features:

☐ **Shoulder Padding.** Look for thick, foam-filled pads that will keep the pack's shoulder straps from digging into your shoulder muscles.

☐ **Frame Fit.** Try the pack on to see how well its length and width fit your own body size. The frame should feel comfortable with baby in it—no discomfort from the top rail digging into your backbone or from the frame interfering with your arm movements.

☐ **Strap Position.** The straps should hit you directly on top of the soft muscles halfway between your neck and the end of your shoulders. If the straps are too widely set, they will cause undue postural stress. If they are too narrow, they may cause chafing and constriction around your neck area.

☐ **Seat Design.** The crotch of the carrier's seat should be narrow enough that baby's legs are not spread uncomfortably far apart. The leg holes of the seat should be flush with the seat rather than higher than the seat so that the circulation in the baby's legs will not be cut off. The rims of the leg holes should be finished so that they are soft and won't scratch your baby.

☐ **Safety Belt.** The seat should be equipped with a sturdy, easy-to-operate seat belt to prevent the baby from standing up in the carrier.

☐ **Front Bar Padding.** Front rail padding will protect your baby's teeth when she mouths the front bar of the carrier frame as you walk.

☐ **Fabric Strength and Durability.** Look for packs made with sturdy, stretch-resistant fabrics that are easily sponged clean. Check the seams, especially around the top rail of the pack to be sure that they have double or triple stitches at stress points.

☐ **Storage Section.** A small storage compartment at the base of the pack may be a helpful option for long outings.

☐ **Pelvic Bracing.** A pack with a padded pelvic belt can help to redistribute the weight of the pack off your shoulders and onto your less vulnerable pelvic area. This option is well worth the extra expense if you're planning to use the pack for camping or long treks.

☐ **Support Stand.** Some packs come with an attached fold-out stand that makes installing the baby and mounting her on your back simpler. While not a necessity, this feature is a nice option. Note: Because of its instability, *the stand should not be used as an infant carrier*. Examine the hinge mechanism of the stand to be certain it cannot capture or crush tiny fingers in its scissoring action.

GERRY DELUXE KIDDIE PACK

Model 072   Gerico, Inc.

The Gerry Deluxe Kiddie Pack is a durable, well-designed frame pack for the serious hiker as well as the grocery shopper. The pack has an adjustable inner seat with a storage area below. The extra-wide foam shoulder straps and a padded top rail are designed for your comfort and baby's safety. A wide-angle support stand, which stabilizes the carrier while you put your child in it, locks securely in the open position. The pack comes with an adjustable padded hip belt to help redistribute the baby's weight and a headrest to support the smaller baby.

Approximate Retail Price $32

DIAPERS AND TOILET TRAINING AIDS

You'll be changing your baby about 6,000 times in the first two and a half years, so it's worthwhile to put some thought into what kind of diapers you plan to use. The biggest decision you'll need to make is whether to use a diaper service, to buy fabric diapers, or to stock up on disposable diapers.

You can count on your newborn using as many as a hundred diapers a week during the first four months of life. So changing diapers and washing diapers will be two of the most time-consuming tasks you will face.

DIAPER TIME DANGER

A research study by Mary A. McCormick and her associates at the Massachussetts Poison Control System showed that 138 calls to the poison center were received in a three-month period regarding accidents occurring during diapering. Three fourths of the babies involved were between the ages of seven months and eighteen months.

There were 30 different harmful substances eaten or inhaled by these babies during diapering. The main offenders were baby powder, ointments and creams, and baby wipes. The symptoms of the babies depended on the product and included coughing, wheezing, choking, shortness of breath, and vomiting. In most of the cases the babies had grabbed the products from their parents; in the rest of the cases the parents had given the baby the powder container or other product to entertain him while his diapers were being changed. (Based on an article from the *Journal of the American Medical Association*, November 5, 1982, Vol. 248, No. 17, pp. 2159-60.) Keep potentially harmful products out of baby's hands and reach during diapering.

DISPOSABLE DIAPERS

Using disposables is definitely more convenient and less time-consuming than laundering your own cloth diapers. Yet, they are more expensive to use than either laundering your own diapers or using a diaper service. You'll be paying as much as 32¢ per diaper (depending on size), which means an investment of at least $1,300 for the twenty-four to thirty-six months that your baby is in diapers.

Aside from the cost factor, another major drawback to disposables is the fact that they are more likely to cause diaper rash. A survey of one-month-old babies found that 18 percent of babies who wore cloth diapers had diaper rash; 33 percent of the babies who wore cloth with plastic diapers had diaper rash; and 54 percent of the babies who continually wore paper diapers had diaper rash. (Fred Wiener, "The Relationship of Diapers to Diaper Rashes in the One-Month-Old Infant," *Journal of Pediatrics*, 95:3, September, 1979, pp. 422-24.)

We feel that **Huggies** are the number-one choice for disposable diapers because of their superior tapes and better fit. **Luvs** are our second choice, and **Pampers** come in last because of poorer performance of tapes and more leakage.

Proctor and Gamble has recently released a new version of Pampers that promises to overcome the diaper's major flaws. The diaper itself has increased absorbency, the double elastic legs promise better fit with less side leakage, and the tapes have been designed to be easy to use and refastenable.

It's wise to steer clear of off-brands of paper diapers since consumer surveys show wide ranges of quality and problems such as poorly adhering tapes, leakage, and poor paper performance.

DISPOSABLE DIAPER CHECKLIST

☐ **Sample Different Brands.** Rather than buying caseloads of disposables before you bring your baby home, it's a smart idea to sample a variety of brands in the newborn size until you find one that fits well and has the softness and quality you're looking for. Name brands seem to have a more consistent quality than generic or house brand disposables.

- [ ] **Compare Prices.** Disposables can vary widely in price, so it's wise to find discount stores and to buy your chosen brand by the case. Our price check varied from 19 cents to 32 cents per diaper (newborn sizes are the least expensive; toddler the most expensive).

- [ ] **Inspect Each Diaper.** Before you put a disposable diaper on your baby, check it over to be sure that there are no impurities, discolorations, or foreign materials in the paper padding.

- [ ] **Check for Clumping.** Avoid brands that shred or bunch up when they become wet, since your baby could be harmed by ingesting loose paper pieces from such diapers.

- [ ] **Create Air Holes.** Part of the reason for increased diaper rash with disposable diapers is the lack of air circulation under the plastic. Also, parents aren't as likely to pick up the cues that their baby is wet and needs to be changed. As a remedy to this situation, pinch out a small piece of the plastic liner in the baby's seat area before putting it on him in order to allow air in and to let you know when baby is really wet.

- [ ] **Fit.** Look for the weight and size charts on the side of the box to help you in selecting the proper size for your baby's needs. Elastic legs on disposables are a luxury rather than a necessity, but have become increasingly popular because they help prevent leakage.

☐ **Dispose Properly.** Don't try to flush a disposable in the toilet, even without the plastic; the paper lining plugs up the plumbing. Roll the diaper into a tight ball, taping it to itself, and put it into a plastic-bag-lined garbage receptacle. When you're ready to throw out used diapers, seal up the trash bag with a twist tie so there's no danger of contamination to people who handle your garbage.

☐ **Receptacle.** You will need a large-size trash can for disposing of used diapers. A large **Rubbermaid Roughneck** garbage can is a good buy with its rectangular shaped mouth—exactly the right size for holding a garbage bag open by stretching it across the can's lip. The can's locking latches on either side can help to keep curious tots out.

☐ **Tapes.** Diapers with refastenable tapes are an extra convenience; or you can keep a small roll of strapping tape or masking tape and a pair of safety-tipped scissors handy for when diaper tapes fail or if you want to refasten the nonrefastenable tapes.

FABRIC DIAPERS

You can purchase fabric diapers in either

flat, prefolded, or fitted styles. *Flat* diapers are a single, large piece of cloth to be folded by you into the shape you prefer (usually a triangle or rectangle). Most parents like to put extra folds in the center section where baby wets. *Prefolded* diapers are stitched into a rectangular shape with extra layers already sewn into the center section. *Fitted* diapers are constructed to adjust to your baby's crotch section and usually come in a figure-eight shape.

The most common diaper fabrics are gauze, bird's eye, and flannel. Gauze is the most airy and lightweight. Bird's eye is a smooth fabric, similar to dish towel material, that is woven with a pattern of small diamonds. Flannel is usually thick with a soft nap to it. Bird's eye is the most absorbent of the three fabrics while flannel appears to be the most comfortable next to baby's skin.

FABRIC DIAPER CHECKLIST

☐ **Amount.** Start out with three dozen diapers. You may want to purchase more once the baby is home and you can tell more about your laundry schedule.

☐ **Weight.** Fabric diapers usually come in sets of a dozen. Compare diapers if you have a choice and select the heavier weight package.

☐ **Folding.** We would suggest the prefolded style of diaper simply because it is much easier to use than the larger unfolded styles that take additional time to fold each time you use them.

- [ ] **Size.** Although your baby will be very tiny at first, it's smart to buy a regular-size diaper that can be used throughout babyhood and simply adapt it to your new baby's smaller size by folding it double.

- [ ] **Diaper Pins.** You will need several pairs of diaper pins, preferably with safety locks that snap down over the metal latch section of the pin to prevent accidental opening. Avoid plastic-head pins that are brittle and frequently break, exposing the baby to puncture wounds.

- [ ] **Waterproof Pants.** Waterproof pants are important for keeping baby's bedding and clothing dry. Those that snap on are easier to use than the pull-up designs and they offer more air circulation—an important feature in preventing diaper rash. Buy at least three pairs in the newborn size.

- [ ] **Diaper Liners.** Diaper liners are a relatively new product designed to help keep babies dryer. These disposable inserts are especially handy for night diapering and allow you to dispense with "double diapering" to control dampness through the night. **Soft Care Diaper Liners** are good for fabric diapers and **Diaper Doublers** are disposable insert pads for either cloth or disposable diapers.

DIAPER SERVICE

Diaper services are an excellent compromise between buying your own fabric diapers and investing in two years' worth of disposable diapers. Besides being less expensive than disposable diapers, they tend to be more diaper-rash resistant because of the high temperatures and strong detergents that commercial launderers can use.

Most diaper services allow you to choose the diapers that will be exclusively your baby's for the time that you use the service. Fresh diapers are dropped off at your home once or twice a week and soiled diapers are taken away in a mesh bag supplied by the service. Usually a diaper pail is also supplied. Call your diaper service and reserve the number of diapers you want delivered before your baby is home.

CURITY PREFOLDED DAY/NIGHT DIAPERS

Model 110—00   The Kendall Company

Curity Prefolded Day/Night Diapers are superabsorbent, made with an open-weave gauze fabric with a fiber sponge lining sewn inside. The diapers, which measure 14″ × 20½″ are prefolded with a seven-layer center panel. The panel dries as quickly as other prefolded diapers. The diapers are 100 percent cotton and the sponge liner is polyester.

Approximate Retail Price   **$12/doz.**

CURITY UNFOLDED CLOTH DIAPERS

The Kendall Company

Curity Unfolded Cloth Diapers can be folded to whatever size best fits your baby, and they launder more thoroughly since there are no seams or pockets to hold residual bacteria that promote diaper rash. The disadvantage is that you have to fold them each time you diaper your baby. These diapers measure 21" × 40" and by folding in quarters you can make a thick, four-layer panel in the center where baby wets. They're made of 100 percent cotton gauze.

Approximate Retail Price   **$12/doz.**

DENBI DIAPERS

Denbi Products, Inc.

Denbi Diapers combine a diaper and waterproof pants. They are contoured to fit well and come in newborn, medium, large, and toddler sizes. The Velcro self-fastening tabs on each side eliminate the need for diaper pins. The inner, diaper part of the product is made of 100 percent cotton while the outer layer is waterproof. A fiber padding has been added in the center of the diaper to improve absorbency. They are sold singly or three per pack.

Approximate Retail Price   **$8/3 pack**

DUNDEE PRE-FOLDED BIRDSEYE DIAPERS

Dundee Mills Baby Products Division

The Dundee Pre-Folded Birdseye Diapers are made of 100 percent cotton bird's eye. They feature double layers of cotton on the side panels and a triple thickness in the center. These diapers are also available for a somewhat higher price with a superabsorbent polyester liner in the center panel.

Approximate Retail Price   **$10/doz.**

DUNDEE REDI-FOL® PRE-FOLDED DIAPERS

Dundee Mills Baby Products Division

Dundee Redi-Fol® Pre-Folded Diapers measure 14½″ × 20½″. They are made of 100 percent cotton gauze, have reinforced edges for longer wear, and are folded in such a way that there are six layers in the center and four on the side panels. These diapers are also available for a somewhat higher price with a superabsorbent polyester liner in the center panel.

Approximate Retail Price   **$14/doz.**

BABY POWDER RISK

Baby powder can be dangerous because it can cause a rare form of pneumonia when it is inhaled in quantity by a baby. Never give your baby an open baby powder can to play with.

DIAPERING ACCESSORIES

CHANGING TIME CHANGING PAD

Sassy

Changing Time Changing Pad is a foamy plastic changing pad that wipes clean, folds up, and gets stuffed into its own carrying case. It's great for throwing in your diaper bag for emergency diaper-changing times.

Approximate Retail Price $7

GERRY FLIP-TOP DIAPER PAIL

Model 475   Gerico, Inc.

The Gerry Flip-Top Diaper Pail from Gerico has a foot-activated release mechanism that allows you to open the pail, but only when the handle is in the down position. When the handle is in the up position, the pail can be locked to keep a curious tot out. The pail's 26-quart capacity holds up to 60 diapers at a time. The directional pouring spout and recessed hand-holds at the base of the pail make it easy to use. Its square shape allows it to fit flush against the wall.

Approximate Retail Price $6

DIAPER DUCK
F & H Products

The Diaper Duck from F & H Products hooks over the toilet seat to hold on to your baby's soiled diaper while the toilet is flushing. Pull the diaper back through the device to squeeze out the excess water. The diaper duck is made of a tough, durable

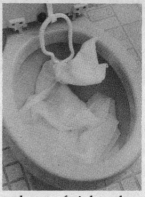

material and can be stored out of sight when not in use.

Approximate Retail Price $6

SANDBOX CHANGER
Sandbox Industries

The Sandbox Changer is a deep, roomy diaper bag with adaptable straps that can be snapped onto your stroller (but be sure it will not cause your stroller to become unbalanced), or

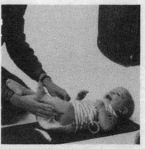

used as a shoulder bag. A detachable changing pad on the side of the bag is useful for out-of-home trips.

Approximate Retail Price $37

116

CHANGING TABLES

A changing table or dressing table should be a safe place to dress your baby or change your baby's diapers. It is one piece of equipment that you will begin using as soon as you bring baby home from the hospital, and it can vary greatly in form and design.

FEATURE CHECKLIST

When shopping for a changing table, look for the following features:

☐ **Storage Space.** The shelves on your diapering stand should be easy to reach so that you can stack clothes in them and pull needed things out quickly.

☐ **Safety Belt.** Hundreds of babies are hurt each year in falls from changing tables. Check out the safety belt to be sure that it is wide and easy to operate—and then make a habit of using it.

☐ **Sturdiness.** Does the table wobble when you shake it? If it does, chances are that it's not sturdy enough for the heavy use you will be giving it.

☐ **Covering.** Although the thickness of the foam pad really doesn't matter, the covering does. Be sure the vinyl is thick and has a smooth surface since you're going to be wiping it off over and over again.

☐ **Side Shelf.** It's helpful to have a side shelf for holding diapering aids so you can reach them easily while changing baby.

The changing tables that follow are in alphabetical order; they are not listed in order of preference. We suggest that you purchase a table that has all of the safety features we recommend in our "Feature Checklist."

FISHER-PRICE CHANGING CENTER
Fisher-Price

Fisher-Price Changing Center is a sturdy, molded plastic changing station for baby. It features four drawers to store things away from small, curious hands, and a foam pad to cushion baby. The center of the base  is an open shelf for diapers and other clothing. High sides at the top of the table and a snaptogether safety belt make safety an easy part of using this table. Once baby is toilet trained, the top of the changing table comes off, the sides slide down, and the table becomes a low, sleek chest for a child's room.

Approximate Retail Price   **$97**

DIAPER PAIL DANGER

From 1973 to 1982 there were 26 drownings involving diaper pails. A second hazard associated with diaper pails is the possible ingestion of the chemical deodorizer located in the lid of many diaper pails.

JENNY LIND DRESSING TABLE
Evenflo Juvenile Products Company

The Jenny Lind Dressing Table from Evenflo (formerly Questor) is a sturdy, wood changing table with safety railings on all four sides. The two open shelves make getting supplies easier. The table features a vinyl-covered foam pad and has a wide  safety strap. The dressing table is available in maple, golden oak, or white.

Approximate Retail Price   **$110**

DRESSING KIT
Model 88   Simmons Juvenile Products Co.

The Dressing Kit from Simmons is a solid wood dresser *top* that attaches securely to the top of an existing dresser. It has safety sides all the way  around and comes in a variety of woods to match the furniture you have already chosen. The kit comes with instructions and parts for easy assembling. A ¾-inch foam pad with a safety belt is also part of the kit.

Approximate Retail Price   **$90**

STROLEE SMALL CHANGER

Strolee

The Strolee Small Changer is a portable changing pad with a rigid base that goes across the crib's bars for an instant place to do diapering. It can also be used wherever you want to  change your baby. The changer comes with a quilted pad and a wide safety belt.

Approximate Retail Price   **$25**

TOILET TRAINING

Deciding on the best time to begin toilet training can be a difficult issue for many parents. The time is definitely later than in your mother's day. In the forties and fifties, the "best" mothers were judged by how well they had potty trained their babies by age one. In fact, it was the mothers who were getting trained to stop everything and race their babies to the bathroom.

Now, *around* two years of age seems to be good timing. Child development specialists have found that by that time most children can follow a sequence of actions, can tell you what they want to do, and can associate their body sensations with a needed action.

Although we have reviewed seat adapters

for adult toilets, most tots seem more secure on floor models because their feet can touch the ground, and they don't have to deal with the fear of being flushed down the toilet. Then again, some children want to be just like brothers and sisters and in that case the adult seat adapter would be a better buy.

It might be a good first step on the self-toileting journey to take your child with you when you shop for potty chairs. Usually children do best with only two choices, so you may want to scout around in advance to select the most desirable purchases.

You will also need to purchase regular children's underwear to mark the transition out of diapers. The thick, bulky training pants are not as good a buy as they might seem. They tend to undergo tremendous shrinkage during washings, and they are so bulky that they feel much like diapers when youngsters are wearing them and they often forget and go back to wetting them.

There's really no need to make toilet training a huge emotional issue. One way to avoid hassles is to lavish praise for successes and mutely overlook failures. A good source for further information on how to carry out your toilet training campaign is *Toilet Training In Less Than a Day* by Azrin and Fox. The book's step-by-step technique is helpful, although you may want to take the book's *blitzkrieg* approach lightly. Another handy paperback book is Vicki Lansky's *Practical Parenting Toilet Training.*

FEATURE CHECKLIST

When shopping for a potty chair, look for the following features:

☐ **Smooth Finish.** Feel the edges of the potty with your fingers to be sure that the molded plastic or the wood is smoothly finished and free from sharp edges or splintering.

☐ **Flexible or Absent Splash Guard.** The rings of some potties have razor sharp cups in front, supposedly to keep little boys from splashing over. If there is such an adapter on the front of the potty you plan to buy, check to see that it is flexible and soft and won't hurt tender skin if your youngster bumps up against it getting on or off.

☐ **Top Loading Chamber.** The most convenient chambers to remove for flushing are those that remove easily from the top of the chair. Most children's potties require that you move the seat forward, stoop down, and then jerkily drag the pot across uneven tracks while trying not to spill the contents. A top-loading chamber will eventually allow your child to do the emptying process himself—a definite step toward independence.

☐ **Seat Belts Unnecessary.** Don't worry about seat belts on this product. Most can be readily slipped off and discarded.

☐ **Dual Use.** Some potties are designed to be used on the floor with a removable top ring that adapts to the adult seat—a nice extra that makes the unit more adaptable.

The following product reviews are listed in alphabetical order, not in order of preference. Carefully read our "Feature Checklist," and then choose the potty chair that best suits your needs.

LESS THAN A DAY TOILET TRAINER

Model 79Y   Cosco Inc.

The Less Than A Day Toilet Trainer has a chamber that can be removed from the top and a removable flexible splash guard. The seat comes with a music box that plays music when the weight of the chamber increases—on the theory that the music rewards the child for performing as desired. A facial tissue holder on the side is an unnecessary extra. The potty chair comes with a paperback copy of *Toilet Training In Less Than A Day*.

Approximate Retail Price   **$25**

POTTIE CHAIR/STEP STOOL

Model 750   Kewaunee Equipment Company

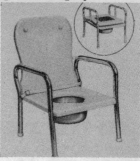

While the Pottie Chair/Step Stool from Kewaunee has a chamber that must be removed from the rear, it does slide easily on its railings. The chair is made of solid wood for durability, it has chrome railings that make backing down to the seat much easier, and it has rubber tips on the legs to prevent slipping. An added plus is that the lid of the seat folds down to make it into a useful bathroom step stool for youngsters. The potty chair has a removable deflector.

Approximate Retail Price   **$22**

SADDLE POTTY

Glenco

The Saddle Potty from Glenco is a modern version of the chamber pot. It is a single-piece unit and is useful for overnight stays and as an auxiliary device to be stored in the trunk of your car for those times when a filling station is not in sight.

Approximate Retail Price   **$4**

TAKE-ALONG POTTY SEAT

Practical Parenting

The Take-Along Potty Seat has a simple design that folds down into a neat 5-inch square, flat piece so that you can tuck it in your glove compartment or pocketbook when shopping or traveling. The adapter fits any standard toilet and is made of washable plastic. It is currently available through mail order only (see our "Manufacturers Directory") and the price includes shipping.

Approximate Retail Price   **$5.50**

TOPPER TOILET SEAT

Crawl Space, A Division of Con-Serv, Inc.

The Topper Toilet Seat can quickly adapt your adult toilet seat to child size with this attachable toilet ring. The base of the ring fastens to the back of the adult seat with adhesive backing. The ring has a clip-on hook so it will stay in the up position when adults want to use the toilet. The Topper eliminates the fear of falling in and there are no chambers to empty or clean.

Approximate Retail Price   **$15**

BOTTLES AND OTHER FEEDING PRODUCTS

Feeding your newborn is an intimate experience for you and your child, and using the appropriate products can enhance this special time. Some products must be chosen jointly with your baby's doctor; others are a matter of preference or practicality.

FORMULAS

The best way to choose your baby's formula is to consult with the doctor you plan to use after giving birth to your baby. Infant formulas are used because regular cow's milk is not suitable for babies under the age of one. Its sugars and proteins are not balanced correctly for baby digestion.

Formulas can be purchased in powder form that you reconstitute yourself, in premixed cans that are either ready-to-feed or need to be diluted, and in throw-away bottles, complete with nipples. Powdered formulas you mix yourself are far cheaper than premixed liquids; most of what you are paying for in the premixed liquid is water. Formula sold in a throw-away baby bottle is the most expensive, but because of the convenience factor it may come in handy for trips or for babysitters.

Discuss with your baby's doctor how to prepare your baby's formula so that you will know what equipment to buy. Some doctors insist on sterilized bottles and formula so that bacteria are killed. Others suggest that you simply use caution about refrigerating formula, using it up quickly and not reusing bottles that haven't been emptied. Since different physicians give different instructions about preheating bottles, too, it's best to know what you're doing before you bring the baby home.

After your doctor gives you a brand name for your baby's formula, we suggest that you shop around for the best prices for this relatively expensive item. Discount drug and department stores and large chain stores like **Toys 'R' Us** often carry popular formula brands at a considerable savings. And buying formula by the case will not only lower the cost, but will also save on trips to the store.

BOTTLES

There are two types of bottle feeding systems. The more common system is the standard baby bottle that usually comes with a nipple, a screw-on top, and a small sealer valve to close off the bottle when you invert the nipple for sanitary storage. The alternative to the standard bottle is a bottlelike frame into which special plastic bags are inserted. These systems use wide-necked nipples that attach at the top of the frame and hold the bag filled with formula in place.

Standard baby bottles save you money because you continually recycle them. They are usually made of glass, clear plastic, or opaque plastic. The advantage of glass bottles is that they are easily cleaned and they don't retain any milk odor. But they do break when dropped. Clear plastic bottles are more lightweight than glass and are also break-resistant.

The main problem with opaque bottles is that you can't see the contents. You don't know if you are aiming the nipple right for baby's needs. Opaque bottles also tend to be more porous and can stain from juices and retain odors if they are not cleaned thoroughly. Avoid bottles shaped like bears, ice cream cones, or other figures. They're simply too difficult to clean.

With all of these considerations in mind, the best purchase for your baby would be the standard baby bottle made of clear, unbreakable plastic.

NIPPLES

In addition to standard rubber nipples, there are nipples with holes especially designed for cereal and juices, "orthodontic" nipples (**Nuk** is a brand name for a popular orthodontic nipple), and molded silicon (clear) nipples. Orthodontic nipples have a bulbous tip with a protruding rim that is supposed to be positioned at the top of the baby's mouth when she sucks. These nipples have gained immense popularity because of advertisements that claim that the nipple shape mimics the human breast and that the tongue action of the baby is more "normal" as a result. But parents have reported problems with the nipples becoming sticky and rotting, perhaps because they are so difficult to clean on the inside.

We recommend that you let your baby try a regular nipple like those manufactured by **Evenflo** and an orthodontic nipple such as Nuk to see which one is preferred. A standard nipple is easier to clean and doesn't have to be inserted in your baby's mouth in a certain direction. But your baby may prefer the orthodontic nipple because of the fit in her mouth. Actually, either nipple is perfectly acceptable as long as the flow of milk is not so fast that your baby has to use her tongue to try to hold milk back to stop from choking and yet not so slow that she becomes exasperated.

BOTTLE FEEDING SUPPLIES

☐ **Bottles.** You should have four to six 8-ounce clear plastic bottles and two 4-ounce clear plastic bottles. Nipples are usually supplied but you can buy more later as you need them.

☐ **Orthodontic Nipple.** Buy one orthodontic

nipple and let your baby try it before investing in more.

☐ **Bottle/Nipple Brush.** Have one cleaning brush with thick bristles for the bottle on one end and tiny bristles for cleaning the nipple on the other end.

☐ **Sterilizing Equipment.** If recommended by your doctor, get a large, tall pot with a top for sterilizing the baby's bottles. Or, special devices designed to sterilize the bottles are available in the nursery departments of most stores.

☐ **Measuring Equipment.** You will need easy-to-read measuring cups and spoons.

☐ **Pacifier.** Most young babies have a very strong sucking urge that isn't completely met by emptying a baby bottle. A pacifier can help meet that need. It can also help to soothe a baby who's waiting for her bottle to heat up.

☐ **Bottle Warmer.** This is an optional accessory that may prove useful during baby's early months, especially if your bedroom and kitchen are on different floors.

When preparing your baby's formula, remember to always measure carefully; don't succumb to the temptation to make the formula weaker or stronger. And always check the date on the package to be sure that the formula is fresh. Only make enough for a few days at a time and keep it well refrigerated. Never give the baby leftover formula from an unfinished bottle.

BOTTLES

EVENFLO COMPLETE NURSER KIT

Model 40113   Evenflo Juvenile Products Company
The Evenflo Complete Nurser Kit is a pre-packaged set of a variety of bottles and accessories. Included in the kit are two 8-ounce plastic and two 8-ounce glass nursers, a 4-ounce glass bottle, a 4-ounce novelty nurser shaped like a puppy (make sure you clean this *thoroughly*), a selection of four types of nipples (standard, juice, formula, and water) for a variety of liquids, caps, rings and sealing disks, nipple and bottle cleaning brushes, and a pair of tongs.
Approximate Retail Price $12

EVENFLO DELUXE NURSING SET

Model 40302   Evenflo Juvenile Products Company
The Evenflo Deluxe Nursing Set can supply all of your bottle feeding needs. The set comes with a nine-bottle capacity electric sterilizing unit and a lift-out rack. It makes live steam from four ounces of water that you pour into it, and it is equipped with an automatic shut-off device to prevent overheating. Included in the boxed set are two 8-ounce glass and two 8-ounce clear plastic bottles, one 4-ounce glass and one 4-ounce plastic bottle. A pacifier, tongs, bottle/nipple brush, hoods, and disks are also part of the Nursing Set. It is U.L. listed.
Approximate Retail Price $38

GERBER CLEAR PLASTIC NURSER

8 oz.   Gerber Products Company

The Gerber Clear
Plastic Nurser's de-
sign features easy-to-
hold channeled sides
and clear-cut raised
indicators for both
ounces and milliliters.
It is stain and odor re-
sistant and can be
washed in the dish-
washer, on the top
rack.   The bottle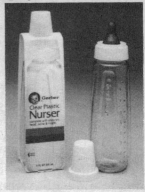
comes with a snap-on hood, collar, and stan-
dard latex nipple.

Approximate Retail Price   **$.88**

NIPPLES

EVENFLO NIPPLES

**Models 21103–21106   Evenflo Juvenile Products
Company**

Evenflo nipples have patented air valves that
are designed to prevent excess air swallowing,
to eliminate nipple pull out, and to help prevent leaking and collapsing during use. The
nipples come in colors that designate use: blue
is for water, yellow for milk, orange with a
cross-cut hole for juice, and amber latex for
formula. These nipples are sold in packages
of three.

Approximate Retail Price   **$1**

INFA PUR NIPPLES

Monterey Laboratories, Inc.

Infa Pur nipples are made of molded silicone material that makes them more durable than latex. They are less likely to build up sticky residue, crack, or collapse than standard nipples. Also, they do not contain nitrosamines, a chemical recently found in latex nipples. The nipples can be boiled or frozen, but unlike latex nipples, the nipple holes cannot be enlarged without damaging the nipples. The nipples are sold two in a package.

Approximate Retail Price   **Standard $1.50**
Orthodontic $2.50

GERBER TRAINER DRINKING SPOUT

Model 76194   Gerber Products Company

The Gerber Trainer Drinking Spout is a rigid plastic screw-on collar that looks somewhat like a nipple. It has large holes in the top and is designed to make the transition from nursing to drinking liquids in a cup easier. It is designed for use with an 8-ounce or 4-ounce bottle. The collar is dishwasher safe. Because of the danger of choking on increased liquid, we recommend this device be used only with older babies and only with close supervision.

Approximate Retail Price $1

SIT 'N SIP

Model 1002   The First Years

The Sit 'N Sip from The First Years is designed for toddlers who prefer to drink sitting up. You place this clear tube inside the bottle (it reaches from the nipple area to the bottom of the bottle) so that baby sucks liquids from the bottom of the bottle 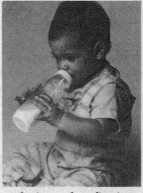 rather than the top. The tube's gasket fits into standard and orthodontic nipples. The Sit 'N Sip can be used in 4- or 8-ounce bottles. It's dishwasher safe and can be boiled for sterilization. A pipe-cleaner-style brush is recommended for proper cleaning.

Approximate Retail Price $1.20

STERILIZERS

GERBER DELUXE ELECTRIC BOTTLE STERILIZER

Model 76040   Gerber Products Company
The Gerber Deluxe Electric Bottle Sterilizer is a U.L. approved model that shuts off automatically when sterilization has been completed. Water is added to the product to produce the sterilizing steam. Bottles can be sterilized in the eight-bottle storage rack, or you can use this unit to sterilize your baby's formula.
Approximate Retail Price **$34**

GERBER NON–ELECTRIC STERILIZER

Model 76046   Gerber Products Company
The Gerber Non-Electric Sterilizer is a stove-top bottle sterilizer set that includes an aluminum pot, a lift-out storage rack with an eight-bottle  capacity, and a lid with a steam vent.
Approximate Retail Price **$15**

BOTTLE ACCESSORIES

EVENFLO ELECTRIC BOTTLE WARMER

Model 41201   Evenflo Juvenile Products Company

The Evenflo electric bottle warmer uses two teaspoons of water to steam-heat the base and sides of a bottle of formula. It is designed for stability and is U.L. approved. The unit automatically turns off when the water has boiled away; the heating element has been recessed underneath a plastic grid. A two-foot electric cord is attached to the bottom of the unit.

Approximate Retail Price $8

GERBER NIPPLE BRUSH and BOTTLE BRUSH

Models 76153 and 76154   Gerber Products Company

The Gerber Nipple and Bottle Brushes have plastic-coated wire handles that can be hung up for storage. Their durable nylon bristles are contoured to effectively clean the bottom and sides of bottles or nipples. Both brushes are dishwasher safe.

Approximate Retail Price   Nipple Brush $ .75
**   Bottle Brush $1.50**

PACIFIERS

INFA PUR PACIFIER

Model 1286   Monterey Laboratories Inc.

The Infa Pur Pacifier is unlike latex pacifiers, which rot over time. This crystal clear pacifier is made of molded silicon that is virtually free of nitrosamines, a chemical found in standard latex nipples. The pacifier comes with a three-year unconditional guarantee.

Approximate Retail Price $1.50

MAM PACIFIER

Sassy

The Mam Pacifier from Sassy is con-toured to encourage natural tongue place-ment and breathing. As the baby sucks, the shield is pulled in-  ward to maintain orthodontic alignment. Top and bottom of the pacifier are identical so you can't put the pacifier into your baby's mouth upside down. The button handle is a safety measure to prevent strangulation; it also allows baby to sleep on her tummy. The soft, latex nipple closely resembles that of a nursing mother. Sassy has also designed a similar model for newborns called the Minimam. The pacifiers are sold two per package.

Approximate Retail Price $3

NUK ORTHODONTIC PACIFIER–EXERCISER
NUK TODDLER SIZE PACIFIER–EXERCISER

Models 02500 and 02516   **Reliance Products Corp.**

The Nuk Orthodontic Pacifier-Exerciser was developed in Germany many years ago by Dr. Adolf Mueller. The pacifier nipple is shaped to imitate the mother's nipple in the baby's mouth. The tonguing action of the baby is similar to breast-feeding. The toddler size pacifier is larger and accommodates babies who are 18 months and older.

Approximate Retail Price   **$1.50**

PACIFIER HAZARDS

Even though many pacifiers have a loop that might suggest they could be tied around a baby's neck, to do so could cause strangulation. If you use a pacifier at nap or bedtime, stitch the pacifier to a rolled up diaper. Also, check pacifiers for any signs of deterioration. A potential hazard exists when deterioration occurs and the nipple can be sucked away from the shield.

FEEDING ACCESSORIES

EVENFLO ELECTRIC FEEDING DISH

Model 41355   Evenflo Juvenile Products Company

The Evenflo Electric Feeding Dish has three compartments for baby's food. Two of the compartments will heat baby's food. The third, nonwarming section, can be used for fruit, gelatin, or other foods. A clear cover comes with this UL approved unit; the cover protects food during the warming process. A suction cup at the base holds the dish in place for feeding. The dish can be immersed for cleaning.

Approximate Retail Price   **$15**

SCOOPER BOWL

Model 3067   Tommee Tippee/Playskool

The Scooper Bowl from Tommee Tippee is a small, bright red bowl, made of unbreakable, scratch resistant plastic. It has a unique curved rim that helps in the process of guiding food onto your baby's spoon. The suction base (with a release tab on the side) keeps the bowl in place during feeding. The bowl is dishwasher safe and sterilizable once the suction rim is snapped off.

Approximate Retail Price   **$2.89**

STAY WARM FEEDING DISH

Model 1614   The First Years

The Stay Warm Feed-
ing Dish from The
First Years keeps
baby food warm with
hot water that is
poured into a reser-
voir in the dish. The
large opening into
which you pour the
water has a permanently mounted stopper.
The plate has three roomy sections for baby's
food and steep sides that make filling the
spoon an easy task. A quick-pull tab releases
the plate's large suction base. The Stay Warm
Feeding Dish is dishwasher safe and break resistant.

Approximate Retail Price   **$6**

THERMAL FOOD BOWL

Model 9100   American Family Scale Company, Inc.

The Thermal Food
Bowl from American
Family Scale has a
sloping bottom that
makes all the food col-
lect on one side,
which you place to-
ward your baby. The
inward sloping of the
lower part of the bowl's rim also helps baby
in self-feeding. Warm water can be poured

into the thermal section through a filling cap, designed to be opened only by an adult. A rubber base helps prevent the bowl from sliding. The bowl is dishwasher safe.

Approximate Retail Price $6

INFA-FEEDER "SOFT-BITE" SPOON

Monterey Laboratories, Inc.

The Infa-Feeder "Soft Bite" Spoon has the widest and deepest part of the spoon's bowl in the front so that the food stays on its tip. The baby uses less spoon in her mouth, which helps to prevent gagging. The spoon's bowl is padded in soft vinyl  to prevent gum injuries. A wide plastic handle makes feeding baby more comfortable.

Approximate Retail Price $1.20

A RESTAURANT SURVIVAL KIT

When taking your tot to a restaurant, the following will be helpful for you and your child:

Small plastic suction dish	*Safety belt or harness*
Lidded cup	*Small toys*
Disposable bib	*Baby food mill*

TRAINING BEAKER

Model 9101   American Family Scale Company, Inc.

The Training Beaker from American Family Scale has uniquely designed handles that make it easy for a toddler to hold on to it with both hands. The mug is the same diameter as a baby bottle, which facilitates the transition from drinking from a bottle to drinking from a cup. The flat bottom is designed to teach a tot to place the mug in the correct position on the table from the very beginning. A training lid helps to prevent spills and it can be removed once the baby masters the art of using the cup. The mug is dishwasher safe.

Approximate Retail Price   **$3.30**

FOODS THAT CHOKE

Be especially careful about feeding your baby foods that might cause choking. Some foods to avoid are nuts, seeds, raw carrot chunks, popcorn, steak pieces, hot dogs, and orange sections.

MAKING YOUR OWN BABY FOOD

Baby's first solid food generally consists of an easily digested, bland, iron-fortified cereal. While there are many theories on when the best time would be to begin feeding cereal to your baby, we strongly recommend discussing this matter with your baby's doctor. Also, you will want your doctor to make a recommendation regarding when you should begin feeding your infant "baby food."

Preparing your baby's food at home rather than buying it in a jar from the supermarket has the advantages of being more flavorful and less diluted than commercial baby foods. You are also able to reduce the amount of fat, sugar, and starches that go into your baby's diet. Home-cooked food is fresher than baby food in jars, especially if the commercially prepared food has been on the grocery store shelves where natural vitamins are destroyed by light and heat.

And making your own baby food is easy. You can use small, hand-operated baby food mills or electric blenders for pureeing vegetables and tender meats for your baby. There's no need to add salt or spices to make it taste better to you—your baby won't know the difference.

The most important thing to remember when preparing your baby's food is cleanliness. Be sure that all of your utensils are cleaned well and rinsed in very hot water. Refrigerate the food immediately and don't keep anything in the refrigerator for more than two days. For longer storage, freeze the prepared food, but do not keep it for more than one month. When using a food mill, read all of the manufacturer's instructions carefully and remember—*keep everything clean*.

FOOD PREPARATION PRODUCTS

HAPPY BABY FOOD GRINDER

Model 800   Bowland-Jacobs International, Inc.

The Happy Baby Food Grinder from Bowland-Jacobs is a superb baby food grinder. It comes with stainless steel cutters and a special spoon and carrying case. Food is placed in the top of the grinder by unfastening the handle and blade assembly. The handle assembly is then screwed back onto the grinder and the lower shaft stand is then used to force food up through the grinding disk. Finely ground food appears in the wide-mouthed cup at the top of the grinder. It processes tender, precooked meats, vegetables, and fruits. Texture of the food is varied by the amount of liquid added. This is excellent for use when taking your toddler to restaurants.

Approximate Retail Price   **$10**

PEAS 'N CARROTS BABY FOOD GRINDER

Sassy

Peas 'N Carrots Baby Food Grinder is a bright yellow grinder that uses a stainless steel straining disc. The large handle makes grinding moist meats, vegetables, and fruits into a smooth puree an easy process. Foods are pushed upward by the pressure of the base and are forced into the top of the mill while the cutter blade handle is rotated. The food grinder is dishwasher safe.

Approximate Retail Price $7

TRAINER FOOD

By the time your baby is sitting up and using her thumb and fingers to pick things up, she is probably ready for feeding herself small chunks of food. Cheerios make a good "trainer food" at the very beginning because they're so easy to pick up and they're just the right size. Other suggestions are small pieces of soft-textured food such as hamburger, chunks of cooked vegetables, macaroni, rice, peanut butter on whole wheat bread, or squares of soft cheese.

BREASTFEEDING PRODUCTS

Many studies have shown human breast milk to be the superior form of nutrition for babies. Its protein is specifically suited to the rapid brain growth of the human baby, it is easy for baby to digest, and it carries immunity factors that protect the baby from illnesses and diarrhea. Breastfeeding also provides a baby with intimate contact with mother while at the same time arousing hormonal responses in the mother's body that enhance maternal, tender feelings. Even if you can only breastfeed for a short period of time, perhaps because you will be returning to work, we recommend that you do so.

Consult with the doctor you plan to use for your newborn for advice regarding whether to breastfeed. The nursing staff at the hospital where you deliver will also be very helpful in educating you about breastfeeding techniques, especially during those first days in the hospital with your newborn. The La Leche League in your area can assist you with any questions or difficulties you may have with breastfeeding; consult your telephone directory for the phone number of the chapter nearest you.

Basically, there are some facts about breast-feeding that will improve your chances of success in nursing your baby. First, the more frequently and the longer period of time your baby nurses, the more milk your body is stimulated to make. And remember, breasts aren't milk *storehouses*, they are milk *producers*, so breast size really has no relationship to milk production capacity.

Human milk doesn't look exactly like cow's milk, so don't be concerned if your breast milk seems bluish or thin in comparison. The cream portion of your milk is not normally given to your baby until the end of a feed.

Breastmilk is a matter of supply and demand. If a baby is only allowed to nurse every four hours, it is likely that your breasts will not produce enough milk to supply him. On the other hand, if you let your baby nurse when he signals you that he is hungry (by crying or nuzzling at your breast), your body's milk production will be adequate for your baby's needs. Different babies have different sleeping patterns that affect their actual feeding rhythms. Nursing a baby when he seems hungry is easier to manage than trying to stall him, while listening to him cry, because you want to impose your schedule on him.

Babies normally go through growth spurts; during these times your baby may seem more fussy and demanding. Most often these growth spurts last about two days and your body responds by increasing milk production. Extra nursing will help calm your baby.

BREAST PUMPS

Babies are by far the most efficient breast pumps; most mothers don't really need to pump their breasts unless they want to store extra milk for times when they aren't at home. There are three kinds of breast pumps: hand-operated pumps that operate with a rubber bulb for suction; manual pumps that work on a piston or syringe cylinder concept; and electric pumps, often used by hospitals.

The rubber bulb pumps (resembling bicycle horns) are most commonly found in drugstores. They are often ineffective in actual use. The kind of action that should be used with this type of pump is a very gentle tugging rather than a solid, unrelenting suction. Even when used correctly, many women complain about bruising and sore tissues from the rigid sharp edge of the pump.

Within the past few years a whole generation of new and very effective breast pumps have evolved that make use of a piston or syringe suction. As with the bulb pump, the milking action should not be a steady suction; it's a gentle, intermittent tugging. The best purchase is a pump that comes with adapters for different breast sizes and with collection bottles that can also be used for storage.

Electric breast pumps are very effective for collecting milk, but they are also so expensive that usually only hospitals or breastfeeding support groups can afford to purchase them. In some cities, costly electric pumps can be rented by individuals on a month-to-month basis. Renting an electric pump would seem wisest when you have a hospitalized premature baby who would thrive better on your milk than on commercial formulas. The pump then serves, too, to keep your milk supply up until the baby comes home.

INFA COMPLETE BREAST PUMP & MILK STORAGE SYSTEM

Model INF–715   Monterey Laboratories, Inc.

The Infa Complete Breast Pump & Milk Storage System from Monterey Laboratories is a total system for pumping and storing breast milk. This kit features a cylinder-style manual pump that allows you to operate it with a gentle tugging action. The collection necks are angled so that the milking action is similar to that of a nursing baby. Two different size nipple adapters come with the kit as do two storage cylinders and two nipples—one regular and one orthodontic. Freezer bags, twist ties, and labels are also supplied for use in freezing your milk.

Approximate Retail Price   **$12.50**

LLOYD–B PUMP

Lopuco, Ltd.

The Lloyd-B Pump is considered one of the
most efficient of the nonelectric pumps. It operates with a hand grip similar to a pistol. A
small valve allows you to control the amount
of suction. Milk flows downward into a glass
collection bottle. The pump is lightweight and
can be sterilized. It comes with a glass shield
and a plastic shield.

Approximate Retail Price   **$40**

CHOOSING A NURSING BRA

There are generally two types of nursing
bras available: those that fasten and unfasten
with hooks or other fasteners in the front-cen-
ter of the bra; and those that have fold-down
flaps that fasten at the top of each cup with a
small plastic latch. Most mothers prefer the
bras with fold-down cup flaps because they
are less cumbersome to operate.

Determining the best size for your nursing
bra isn't always easy. Your breasts will become
noticeably larger during the latter part of your
pregnancy. You may want to purchase nursing bras and break them in toward the end of
your pregnancy when your breasts are likely
to be as large as they will become during the
breastfeeding process.

To measure for a nursing bra, put a tape
measure around your chest, directly under
your arms and above your breasts. This mea-

surement will be the bra size. If your measurement is an odd number, your bra size will be one inch larger. Cup size is measured at the fullest part of your breast. The following will help you determine your cup size:

If your bust measurement is less than 1½ inches larger than your chest measurement, your cup size is | A

If your bust measurement is 1½ to 2½ inches larger than your chest measurement, your cup size is | B

If your bust measurement is 2½ to 3½ inches larger than your chest measurement, your cup size is | C

If your bust measurement is 3½ to 4½ inches larger than your chest measurement, your cup size is | D

Your breast size may change over the process of your breastfeeding.

You will want to purchase as many as six bras since milk leakage is likely to be a problem in the early months of breastfeeding and dampness can encourage the development of bacteria. For that reason, bras should be changed frequently.

FEATURE CHECKLIST

When shopping for a nursing bra, look for the following features:

- ☐ **Comfort.** Choose a bra that expands as you breathe with no binding seams, especially around the breast itself. Faulty-fitting bras can cause plugged ducts in the breast.
- ☐ **Washability.** You should be able to machine wash and dry the bras that you purchase. But since heat is the major destroyer of elastic materials, either wash them on the gentle cycle in a special laundry bag for lingerie or hand-wash them. Dry bras on the lowest heat setting in the dryer or hang them up to dry.
- ☐ **Ease of Use.** Look for bras with fasteners that can be easily opened and closed with one hand, since invariably you will have your baby on one arm.
- ☐ **Strap Adjustment and Comfort.** If you have large breasts you will want to pay particular attention to bra straps. They should be wide and soft so that your shoulders will feel no chafing or binding from the weight of your breasts. When you try the bra on, be sure that the straps will adjust perfectly to your needs. If the bra hikes up in the back while you are wearing it, readjust the straps.
- ☐ **Additional Support.** Some mothers feel more comfortable if their bras offer additional underwiring or latex side support, while others prefer bras that are less noticeable to the wearer. One option is to try several different types of bras at the store, and then to purchase more than one of the type that seems the most comfortable.

ADJUSTABLE CUP NURSING BRA

Model 50　Mary Jane Company

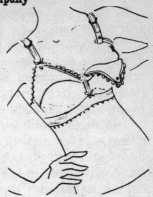

The Adjustable Cup Nursing Bra from Mary Jane has a ladderlike hook-and-eye adjustment that allows this bra to expand to 3 different sizes at times of engorgement or when breasts are larger than usual. The cups are lined with a soft cotton fabric. The outside of the cup is covered with a seamless-look nylon tricot fabric.

Approximate Retail Price　　　　　**$16**

TRICOT NURSING BRA

Model 418　Leading Lady

The Tricot Nursing Bra from Leading Lady is made of soft, nylon tricot. This bra is comfortable but at the same time gives excellent support. The cups have a special snap-open latch called a "Fastnur" that pops out easily when you press your thumb under it.

Approximate Retail Price　　　　　**$11**

BRA PADS

In the early nursing months both breasts will spurt milk even though baby is nursing on only one side. Or your milk can let down at unexpected times. Commercially produced bra pads for nursing mothers can help. These pads are usually found in maternity shops or in the maternity section of department stores.

The most economic and comfortable purchase is layered fabric pads that can be laundered and reused. Disposable paper pads are more expensive in the long run and they can contribute to sore nipples because they frequently have plastic liners that hold moisture up against the breast. But since they don't have to be laundered, they can be a convenience when traveling.

DENBI WASHABLE NURSING PADS
The Denbi Products, Inc.

Denbi Washable Nursing Pads help to prevent milk leakage from soiling your bra and clothing. They come six to a package and are 100 percent cotton and completely washable. Their construction absorbs moisture while allowing air to circulate through the pad.

Approximate Retail Price **$4.50**

LEITE PADS

Tamara Dee, Inc.

Leite Pads from Ta-
mara Dee are wash-
able nursing pads
with several layers of
100 percent cotton
specially woven for
absorbency. They
have a protective ny-
lon backing that al-
lows the pad to breath
yet prevents leakage
onto your clothing.

Leite Pads are available in packages of six.
Approximate Retail Price   **$4.50**

EVENFLO NATURAL MOTHER NURSING PADS

Model 52106   Evenflo Juvenile Products Company

Evenflo Natural Mother Nursing Pads are disposable pads that have 20 absorbent layers
stitched together with an outer layer of special
fabric that breathes yet protects clothing from
leakage. These pads absorb 3 times their
weight in moisture. They come 36 to a box.
Approximate Retail Price   **$3.40**

BATHING ACCESSORIES

The first bath-time experience with your newborn may not be the enchanting, intimate experience you would anticipate. In fact, you'll soon discover that your infant has a positive aversion to being bathed. The reason for the protests has to do with the primitive temperature control of a brand-new body. Rather than being able to shiver, or even change positions, babies maintain temperature stability by chemical changes in the body.

You don't need to worry excessively about your newborn being too cold or too hot, but you might consider postponing the formal bathing rituals for the first weeks after birth, possibly until the baby's first month when she is more able to cope with rapid body cooling.

During this sensitive period, keep baby clean by sponging her while she is under a blanket or towel. You baby's skin has germ-killing and self-protection properties that make the heavy use of soap totally unnecessary. In fact, even light soaping may only be necessary if your baby spits up a lot or if diaper rash is present. In either event, it is wise to consult with your pediatrician regarding setting up your baby's bath-time regimen.

When you do use soap, you will find that the new pump dispensers designed for liquid soap will allow you to keep one hand on the baby while quickly dispensing the exact amount of soap that you need with the other hand. Mild soaps such as **Johnson & Johnson Baby Soap** or **Neutrogena** are recommended.

After determining how often and when your baby will be bathed, have all of your supplies ready to go and the room you will be using warmed up. Then bring your newborn into the room and proceed with bathing.

As an alternative to using your bathtub, you can bathe baby in the kitchen sink or in a molded plastic bathtub. These bathtubs have undergone a revolution in design in the past few years. Most baby bathtubs now have a slanted support area for the baby to recline on that is covered with a nonslip foam pad.

The disadvantage to using baby bathtubs is the arduous filling process. Once filled, it is extremely difficult to carry the tub from one place to another without spilling water over the side. A simple solution is to place the tub on the counter next to the bathroom sink. While it is also possible to place it directly in your bathtub, you would still have to lean over to bathe your baby and this would defeat one of the major purposes of this type of tub.

No matter what approach you take for bathing your child, **never** leave your child unattended in the bathwater.

FEATURE CHECKLIST

When shopping for a baby bathtub, look for the following features:

☐ **Edges.** Molded edges should be smooth and rounded with no sharp, unfinished areas.

☐ **Support.** A slanted support area for the baby, covered in a nonslip surface such as foam, will make bathing your baby easier and safer.

☐ **Cushion Materials.** Do not purchase all-sponge seats or bath support cushions that can be torn into small pieces and eaten by the baby.

☐ **Sturdiness.** Try twisting the tub to be sure that it stays solidly in shape; a sturdy tub makes transporting water easier.

EEZI BATH

Model 8970   American Family Scale Co., Inc.

With the Eezi Bath baby bathtub from American Family Scale you can use your own bathtub faucets to fill this in-genious baby bathtub  that rides piggyback inside your own—you don't have to lift or carry a heavy water-filled tub. Made of heavyweight plastic, the tub has its own special pull plug for emptying the used water. There are small side pockets to hold soap or shampoo. All bathtubs should be used with constant supervision, and we do not recommend using the tub with a second child in the regular tub at the same time, as suggested on the product's carton.

Approximate Retail Price $18

IN-SINK GENTLE BABY BATH

Model 8910   American Family Scale Co., Inc.

The In-Sink Gentle Baby Bath from American Family Scale is a useful alternative to a baby bathtub. You may want to consider this sink adapter, which allows the kitchen sink to have the features of a baby bath. The gentle angle of the seat helps to support the baby on a foam liner. The Baby Bath is available in yellow or white.

Approximate Retail Price $10

NURSERY NEEDS BABY BATHER

Model 1561   Sanitoy, Inc.

Nursery Needs Baby Bather from Sanitoy has a foam-cushioned recliner to help hold your baby comfortably in place. When the baby can sit without support, the recliner lifts out to create a 30-quart tub for toddlers. A flexible hose allows you to drain the tub without lifting or spilling.

Approximate Retail Price $18

TENDER-CARE BATH

Graco Children's Products, Inc.

The Tender-Care Bath from Graco is the best designed of the baby bathtubs. This tub features a gently sloping back support, padded with soft foam. It's sturdy and easy to carry, and has a special compartment for soap, shampoo, and other bathing supplies.

Approximate Retail Price $9

BABY ANCHOR INFANT BATH SEAT

The Wallace, Davis Co.

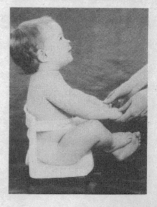

The Baby Anchor Infant Bath Seat from Wallace, Davis is a safe alternative to a baby bathtub. The critical feature of any bath seat for a baby or a tot is that it have a good safety belt for holding your baby in place, as this model does. The four strong

suction cups at the base of the seat keep it
firmly stationed on the floor of your bathtub.
Approximate Retail Price **$12**

SAFETY BEAR BATHTUB SPOUT SAFETY COVER

Family Life Products
The Safety Bear Bathtub Spout Safety Cover
from Family Life Products is a protective covering for your bathtub faucet. A toddler can
get hurt by falling into a sharp or hot faucet
and the Safety Bear Bathtub Spout Safety
Cover has been designed to protect your baby
from such an accident. Shock absorbent and
vinyl coated, it is designed to slip directly over
your bathtub faucet.
Approximate Retail Price **$9**

SASSY BATHING SAFETY KIT

Sassy Inc.
The Sassy Bathing Safety Kit contains a cushioned spout guard designed to look like a great
white whale. It also contains eight fish-shaped
nonskid adhesive treads for the bathtub floor.
The spout cover protects your child from falls
into the spigot and possible burns when the
metal is hot. The treads give a child steady
footing and seating in a slippery tub.
Approximate Retail Price **$10**

SAFETY DEVICES

Baby safety is a critical issue and one that should be of prime importance to parents. Although great strides have been made to make safer *products* for babies, statistics show that the home is still a potentially dangerous place for a baby.

Sometimes seemingly harmless products can be serious safety hazards. Strings have been involved in strangulation deaths, plastic bags in suffocation deaths, and even rubber strips from broken balloons have caused deaths when entrapped in a baby's windpipe. Although obvious factors such as poison, hot appliances, or staircases can cause injury and death, even the furniture in your home can endanger babies. Coffee tables send 87,000 babies a year to hospital emergency rooms.

With the possibility of injury from so many home products, it's easy to see why some parents become concerned about life with a baby. Probably the best step to take is to carefully "baby proof" your house so that the potential dangers have been guarded, and then to never leave your baby unattended during waking hours.

Accordion safety gates constructed out of wood and having X-joints are, in our opinion, *totally unsafe*. They can capture and crush babies' fingers when they are compressed to open. Babies try to climb over them using the lower joints as footholds; this is a safety hazard because babies' necks can become entrapped, causing strangulation. While manufacture of these gates has been halted, they are still available from stores as well as garage sales.

Pressure gates are also less than safe because they can fall down the steps when baby presses up against them, causing more serious injuries to baby than if she fell down without the gate.

The safest gates for guarding stairways, the kitchen, and other rooms that are off-limits to baby are those that have a climbing-resistant mesh with a small diamond pattern. The gate should be firmly attached to the door jam with screws rather than relying on the pressure of rubber gaskets against wood.

The following reviews are of products specifically created to make your child's environment safer. Similar products are grouped together and then listed in alphabetical order.

SAFETY TIP

Despite the charm of having your child's name displayed on sweatshirts, T-shirts, hats, or whatever, it is not a safe idea for your child's name to be visible to strangers. Your child might mistakenly think someone knows him simply because they call him by name.

NURSERY MONITOR

Model 0157   Fisher-Price

With the Nursery Monitor from Fisher-Price you can hear your baby cry even when you are not near the crib. This electronic listening system includes a transmitter and a receiver with an adapter. For increased distance monitoring the receiver uses a 9-volt battery. Volume can be adjusted.

Approximate Retail Price $59

SAFETY MESH BED RAIL

Model 724   Cosco Inc.

The Safety Mesh Bed Rail from Cosco is a nylon mesh panel with a sturdy steel frame; it's one of the safest on the market. The rail is 48 inches long and 16 inches high. Its arms slip under your child's mattress to hold the guard in place. It can also be folded flat for storage. This is helpful when your child has made the transition to a "real" bed.

Approximate Retail Price $18

EASYRIDER

Jagco Enterprises

The Easyrider from Jagco helps keep babies in grocery carts. This nylon mesh belt fastens a baby (six months and older) securely to the seat section of a grocery cart so that she can't stand up or fall out.

Approximate Retail Price $4

MY PAD

Pansy Ellen Products

My Pad from Pansy Ellen has a Velcro self-fastening strap that attaches this pad to the seat of your grocery cart. A click-lock safety buckle on the pad securely fastens your baby so she can't stand or fall out of the cart. The cushion is made of vinyl-

covered foam padding. The unique feature of this pad is that it can also double as a diaper changing pad. It's lightweight and can be easily tucked in your purse or diaper bag. It comes in bright yellow.

Approximate Retail Price   **$7**

TAILORED BABY SAFETY SITTER

Model 2080 H   Tailored Baby, Inc.

The Tailored Baby Safety Sitter is a small, comfy seat that has been designed to hold your baby securely in shopping carts, high chairs, and baby swings. The reversible seat has fur-like fabric on one side and smooth gingham fabric on the other. The seat fastens down with a set of heavy-duty snaps that adjust to your baby's girth.

Approximate Retail Price   **$12**

ZIP-A-BABE HARNESS

Life Manufacturing Company

The Zip-A-Babe harness can be an excellent investment in baby safety. You can use it to hold baby in her chair or in a grocery cart. You can use it to help support a newly walking baby in shopping centers and outdoors where falls could be harmful. This model zips from the back for easy wear and has adjustable shoulder straps for better fit.

Approximate Retail Price $7

PEEDEE DOSE ORAL SYRINGE

Medi-Aid Corporation

The Peedee Dose Oral Syringe helps you give liquid medicine to baby. It is a syringe-type dispenser that allows you to carefully measure the dosage. Then, you simply squirt the medicine directly onto the back of baby's tongue.

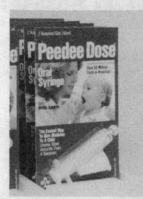

Approximate Retail Price $1.80

ASTROTEMP 9 CLINICAL THERMOMETER

Marshall Electronics, Inc.

The Astrotemp 9 Clinical Thermometer is a battery-operated thermometer that takes only 60 seconds to give a reading. The unit is 5½ inches long

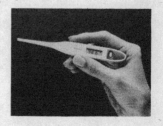

and weighs less than an ounce. The shell is made of unbreakable plastic. The Astrotemp will automatically shut itself off after approximately eight minutes to save the battery, which will operate for more than 300 hours before a change is needed.

Approximate Retail Price   **$19**

GERRY SWING-OPEN SECURITY GATE

Model 505   Gerico, Inc.

The Gerry Swing-Open Security Gate from Gerico is far safer than the old-fashioned accordion gate. This model is molded of rigid, high-impact plastic. The gate is free of rough edges, sharp points, and pinch areas. The small diamond pattern makes it difficult for baby to get a foothold for climbing. The gate is 24 inches high and expands to fit openings from 27 to 42 inches wide. Eyebolts that come with the gate must be installed on both sides of the door to hold the gate. The child-proof latch allows opening and closing by a parent with one hand. The gate has a lift out feature for easy removal.

Approximate Retail Price   **$9**

COOKIE MONSTER CHILD CARRIER

Model 585   Cycle Products Co.

HELMET

Model 730

The Cookie Monster
Child Carrier from
Cycle Products Co.
mounts on the back of
an adult bicycle. Spe-
cial spoke guards pro-
tect baby's legs and
ankles from the dan-
ger of being caught by
spinning   bicycle
spokes. For maxi-
mum   protection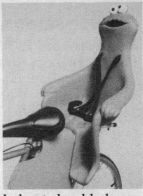
while riding, the safety helmet should always
be worn. Your child should be at least one-
year-old and able to sit alone before using the
carrier. The carrier is also available without the
Cookie Monster design for a slightly lower
price.

Approximate Retail Price   **Carrier $20**
                                      Helmet $40

KINDERGARD CHILD
PROTECTION KIT

Kindergard Corp.

The Kindergard Child Protection Kit is a whole
set of safety aids. The Economy Kit includes:
7 cabinet latches, 15 plugs for electrical outlets,
10 corner cushions for the coffee table and

other sharp-edged tables, and an 8-foot length of cushioned edging for tables. A smaller Trial Kit is also available.

Approximate Retail Price **$14**

CABINET SLIDE LOCK

Model 1402   Sanitoy, Inc.
The Slide Lock for Doors by Sanitoy is an adjustable lock that lets you close cabinets up tight so that baby can't get into them. It's easy for adults to operate, but difficult for a baby. The lock installs easily with no tools.

Approximate Retail Price **$1.80**

REFRIGERATOR SAFETY-CATCH

Dahl House
The Refrigerator Safety Catch from Dahl House is a plastic latch that is attached with two-sided tape to your refrigerator at adult height. With the safety catch in place, the refrigerator door stays shut until *you* are ready to open it.

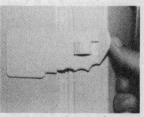

Approximate Retail Price **$1.80**

TOYS

A baby thrives on new experiences. The drive to explore and to learn are almost as strong as the desire to eat or be held. If you watch closely, you will see that much of the first two years of your baby's waking life is filled with countless movements of hands, feet, eyes, and every other body part.

Perhaps for the first time in history, toys are being designed to specifically "fit" babies—the size of their hands, the colors and patterns that attract their eyes, and the novel sounds that capture their attention.

Yet even the most carefully thought-out toy—educational and age-related though it may be—can quickly be cast aside by a baby as boring. That's because over and above the basic educational value of the toy, there is another more abstract quality that is difficult to describe. We call it the *pleasure factor*. Purchasing a toy that your child enjoys and finds fascinating is a satisfying experience.

TOY SAFETY

There is a dark side to toys as products. Unfortunately, not all toys are manufactured with safety in mind. While agencies such as the Consumer Product Safety Commission exist, and do all that they can to alert customers and manufacturers to potential hazards that are present in certain products, you must also do your part to ensure that your child is not injured.

Approximately 130,000 children are injured in toy-related accidents each year. Toys can cut, puncture, burn, shock, or choke a baby. The most serious injuries to babies from toys occur when a baby is left alone for long periods of time to be content with a toy, when the toy is not installed or used correctly, or when babies are allowed to play with toys not appropriate for their ages and skill levels.

If you have any questions regarding toy safety, recall or repair programs, or if you wish to report a problem that you have observed with a toy (or any child-related product) call the Consumer Product Safety Commission hotline at one of the following numbers: **1-800-638-CPSC;** or from Alaska, Hawaii, Puerto Rico, and the Virgin Islands, **1-800-638-8333.** They will be happy to help you.

AGE APPROPRIATE BABY TOYS

Birth to three months
  Mobile
  Small stuffed toys
  Squeaky toys
Three to six months
  Rattle
  Teething ring

Activity center
Crib gym (remove at 5 months)
Six to nine months
Rag doll
Shape sorting toy
Suctioned rattle
Nine to twelve months
Hand-sized ball
Stacking toy
Play telephone
Mirror toy
Twelve months to two years
Shape sorting box
Ride-on toy
Push and pull toy
Music making toy
Indoor sliding board

TOY BUYING CHECKLIST

The following checklist will help you to weed out potentially dangerous toys.

☐ **Correct Age Range.** Abide by the manufacturer's recommended age guidelines that appear on the package. When a guideline states that a toy should only be used by a child two years or older, the actual meaning is that the toy could be *hazardous* when used by a younger child. The suggested age range for a toy is based on safety considerations.

☐ **Developmental Level.** Choosing a toy that is too sophisticated will only frustrate your child. At the same time, a toy that is too simple will only be tossed aside.

- [ ] **Durability.** The toy should be sturdy. Try pulling at the eyes of a stuffed animal; on any toy pull the buttons, wheels, parts, and pieces that could conceivably get trapped in a baby's windpipe if inhaled or swallowed. Be sure that they are secure and won't come off when used.
- [ ] **Small Pieces.** Check rattles, especially small bar bell, safety pin, clothespin, or telephone-receiver-shaped ones to be sure that they could not become lodged in a baby's throat, if fallen on. Be sure that no part of the end is small enough to fit into baby's mouth. Don't buy toys with small parts that can be pulled off.
- [ ] **Rounded Corners and Dull Edges.** Run your finger around the edges of metal trucks and cars or plastic toys to be sure that there aren't any sharp seams or edges that could cut a baby's fingers.
- [ ] **No Exposed Hardware.** There should be no exposed screws or other protruding small parts that might hurt a baby.
- [ ] **No Hinges or Scissoring Action.** Avoid hinges and scissorlike devices, like those on dump trucks, that could crush, pinch, or cut small fingers.
- [ ] **No Projectiles or Points.** Avoid darts, plastic bullets, or other objects that when propelled could cause eye injury.
- [ ] **Nonelectric.** Electrical toys should be avoided for babies and toddlers since they may try to chew on the batteries or become

injured in the process of plugging in a toy. Avoid toys that use heating elements.

☐ **Nontoxic Paint.** Most paints now used on toys are nontoxic. Be cautious about old toys that may have lead-based paint on them.

The toys that follow are listed according to age range (and then alphabetical order within that range), not according to preference. When shopping for a toy for your child, look for toys that match your child's age range. Most manufacturers will mark the age for which the toy is geared on the package.

LULLABY RAINBOW
Model 1512   Tomy Corporation
(Birth to 18 months)
The Tomy Lullaby Rainbow does not suspend above the baby's head, but attaches firmly across the crib from one side to the other. The mobile offers a variety of visually stimulating motions. A colorful musical unit plays "Hush My Baby" as it travels slowly from side to side while the sun moves in and out and the eyes of the cloud open and close. Below the cloud a basket and balloon twirl around. The mobile automatically adjusts when a crib side is raised or lowered. Reminder: remove this or any mobile when your child can reach for it.
Approximate Retail Price $23

SPINNER RATTLE

Model 9531   Johnson & Johnson
(Birth to 18 months)
The Spinner Rattle from Johnson & Johnson
is a break-resistant rattle that contains a race-
track of small red beads and a spinner of
stripes and stars. Babies enjoy the flexible ring
of the rattle for teething and it's easy to grasp.
Approximate Retail Price $6.50

KICKERS

Red Calliope
(2 to 5 months)
Kickers from Red Calliope are stuffed animal
creatures in brightly patterned washable fabrics. They come with grosgrain ribbons to tie
across a playpen or crib. They're especially en-
joyed by babies who are learning how to kick
their feet. Once the child can reach for it, remember to remove it from the crib.
Approximate Retail Price $18

SPLASH AND STACK RECALL

*In the Fall of 1984 Fisher-Price announced a recall
and replacement of their Splash and Stack Bluebird
toy, Model 167, because of a potential suffocation
hazard associated with the cup-shaped head on the
toy. The head can be returned to Fisher-Price, Department 167, 636 Girard Ave., East Aurora, NY
14052. Fisher-Price will replace the head and reim-
burse you for postage.*

SHIRT TALES MUSICAL MOBILE

Model 143–020   Nursery Originals/Division of Century Products, Inc.
(2 to 5 months)

The Shirt Tales Musical Mobile from Nursery Originals has fuzzy creatures in T-shirts rotating around as they hang on to colored plastic balloons that rattle. Soft music plays as they turn. Animals are angled to look down toward baby. Reminder: remove this or any mobile when your child can reach for it.

Approximate Retail Price   **$27**

ACTIVITY CENTER

Model 1134   Fisher-Price
(3 to 18 months)

The Activity Center from Fisher-Price is now a baby classic. It's made of sturdy, break-resistant plastic. This all-in-one toy can be fastened to a crib, or a toddler can carry it around by the top handle. The face of the center of the toy offers a variety of sights, hand actions, and sounds including a squeezer, a clacker, a button-activated bell, a small mirror, a spinner, and a telephone dial.

Approximate Retail Price $12

BALLS IN A BOWL

Model 9531   Johnson & Johnson (6 to 30 months)

Balls in a Bowl from Johnson & Johnson has three clear plastic balls that can be put into and taken out of a large, yellow transparent bowl. Each ball contains a decorated, rotating spin-  ner that makes it interesting as a toy by itself. The entire set is sturdy and break resistant.

Approximate Retail Price $10

FIVE KEYS

Model A–1024   Just for Kids! (6 months and up)

Five Keys from Just for Kids! has a curved display board that houses five different surprises that only operate when baby puts in the right key. Activities include clanking, squeaking, peek-a-boo kittens, a bunny that bounces, and a hen with two twirling eggs. Four rubber feet underneath hold the unit in place. This is a great shape-matching toy.

Approximate Retail Price **$25**

SPINNING BUTTERFLY

**Model 432   Fisher-Price
(6 to 24 months)**

The Spinning Butter-
fly from Fisher-Price
has a butterfly with a
mirrorlike reflector
that spins inside the
clear plastic globe of
this intriguing rattle.
The sturdy suction
cup base enables the
rattle to be fastened
on a high chair tray,
table, or other smooth
surface for batting fun.

Approximate Retail Price   **$4.50**

FIT 'N FILL

**Model 2605   The First Years
(9 months to 3 years)**

The Fit 'N Fill clear
pail from the First
Years comes with a
bright yellow handle
and six blocks in dif-
ferent shapes and
colors. The snap-on

lid has holes in the same shapes so children learn to sort by color and shape.

Approximate Retail Price $6

WALK-ALONG BLOCK WAGON

Model 62024   CBS Toys
(9 months to 3 years)

The Walk-Along Block Wagon from CBS Toys is a long-lasting hardwood wagon. It's a walker wagon for a toddler when the handle is adjusted to the straight-up position. For older preschoolers the handle comes down and it's a pull wagon. Wide wheels also add to the wagon's stability. The wagon comes with 24 bright hardwood blocks.

Approximate Retail Price $20

ROCKING PUPPY

Model 135   Fisher-Price
(12 months to 2½ years)

The Rocking Puppy from Fisher-Price is designed to be stable for the toddler who is just learning how to mount a ride-on toy. The rockers are extra long and have safely rounded edges for protection from falls. Its ears are made of soft fabric and each ear has a sturdy red handle for gripping.

Approximate Retail Price   **$18.50**

CORN POPPER

**Model 768   Fisher-Price
(12 months to 3 years)**

The Corn Popper from Fisher-Price is a favorite of toddlers because they love the popping sound that the Corn Popper makes as they push it in front of them. Inside the clear plastic dome, colored balls pop and fall as the wheels of the toy are moved.

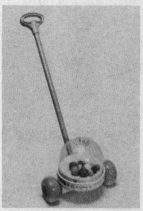

Approximate Retail Price   **$7.50**

X RAYING SWALLOWED PLASTIC TOYS

Mattel Corp. has developed a nontoxic plastic that will show up on X rays. Children ingest thousands of toys every year that are not detectable on normal X-ray equipment. Often location and removal of the object is critical. This development is expected to be in widespread use by major toy manufacturers soon.

LITTLE RED RIDER

Model 0490   Little Tikes
(12 months to 3 years)
The Little Red Rider
from Little Tikes is a
sleek, sturdy first rid-
ing vehicle. The wide
wheelbase and the
low center of gravity
help to prevent tip-
ping. The saddle seat
has a high back for
better support. The
steering wheel comes
with a horn.

Approximate Retail Price   **$21**

STACK 'N SPIN TOP

Model 014   Schaper Manufacturing Co.
(12 months to 3 years)
The Stack 'N Spin Top
from Schaper has four
large colored disks of
different shapes and
sizes that fit on top of
its post. Each piece
can be played with
separately or they can all be fastened onto the
top for spinning fun.

Approximate Retail Price   **$5.50**

BATHTIME WATER WORKS

Model 9583   Johnson & Johnson
(12 months to 4 years)
Bathtime Water Works from Johnson & Johnson has four different toys that come stacked on a raftlike base that floats on water. Included in the set are a paddlewheel spinner, a bright blue water squirter, and two cups.

Approximate Retail Price $13

BIG BABY ROLLER

Model A–1215   Just for Kids!
(12 months and up)
The Big Baby Roller from Just for Kids! is a stable ride-on toy. It's great for the first ride-on toy your child uses. It has triple wheels that give a well-balanced, stable ride. The round steering wheel has a tooting horn and the seat lifts up to store small toys.

Approximate Retail Price $48

BALLOON JEOPARDY

Of all children's products, balloons are the leading cause of suffocation deaths, according to the Consumer Product Safety Commission. Balloons are designed to prevent the passage of air out of the balloon; if a balloon is inhaled, it will be just as effective at preventing the passage of air into the throat.

BUSY POPPIN' PALS

Model 72802   CBS Toys
(over 18 months to 3 years)

Busy Poppin' Pals
from CBS Toys can be
either Sesame Street
or Disney characters
that pop up when lids
are unlocked by five
different knobs and
dials. The unit has a built-in carry handle. This
is not recommended for use in a crib.

Approximate Retail Price   **$14**

PLAY SLIDE

Model 4108   Little Tikes
(18 months to 4 years)

The Play Slide from
Little Tikes is de-
signed with the tod-
dler in mind. This
slide has a gentle an-
gle and a wide-based
ladder for stability. It
folds away easily for
storage or carrying.

Approximate Retail Price   **$26**

TODDLERS' GYM

Model 10959 Childcraft Education Corporation
(18 months and up)

The Toddler's Gym from Childcraft Education Corporation is made of hardwood and masonite. This indoor play unit will help your toddler to let off steam during cold or inclement weather. It's made to strict safety standards and features a climb-in tunnel underneath and safety bars on either side of the top of the platform.

Approximate Retail Price   **$90**

PLAY TRANSPORTER

Model 0280 Little Tikes
(24 months to 7 years)

The Play Transporter from Little Tikes is more than just a truck. This molded plastic van is made up of five pieces and can become a bridge, a tunnel, and a car with a garage.

Approximate Retail Price   **$14**

MANUFACTURERS DIRECTORY

American Family Scale Co.
3718 S. Ashland Ave.
Chicago, IL 60609
(312) 376-6811

Aprica Juvenile Products
P.O. Box 215
Cerritos, CA 90701-0215
(800) 423-6637
California (213) 404-3773

Bonny Bunting
P.O. Box 17345
Washington, DC 20041
(800) 368-3016 or
(703) 435-3915

Bowland-Jacobs
P.O. Box 306
Yorkville, IL 60560
(312) 553-9559

Carriage Craft, Inc.
1133 Broadway, Rm. 1226
New York, NY 10010
(212) 807-6007

CBS Toys/Child Guidance
41 Madison Ave.
New York, NY 10010
(212) 481-6400

Century Products, Inc.
1366 Commerce Drive
Stow, OH 44224
(216) 686-3000

Child Craft
P.O. Box 444
Salem, IN 47167-0444
(812) 883-3111

Childcraft Education Corp.
P.O. Box 444
Salem, IN 47167-0444
(800) 631-5652 or
(812) 883-3111

Cosco Inc.
Juvenile Products Group
2525 State Street
Columbus, IN 47201
(812) 372-0141

Cosmos Trading, Inc.
12 Edgeboro Road
East Brunswick, NJ 08816
(201) 238-3377

Crawl Space
Division of Con-Serv
1900 Section Road
Cincinnati, OH 45237
(800) 543-8616 or
(513) 531-3300

Curity/Kendall
One Federal Street
Boston, MA 02101
(617) 423-2000

Cycle Products Co.
77 Modular Avenue
Commack, NY 11725
(717) 764-8551

Dahl House
P.O. Box 6896
San Jose, CA 95150
(408) 293-2115

The DenBi Company
P.O. Box 509
Oakland, CA 94604
(415) 839-8711

Dundee Mills
Baby Products Div.
111 W. 40th St.
New York, NY 10018
(212) 840-7200

Evenflo Juvenile Furniture
1801 Commerce Dr.
Piqua, OH 45356
(513) 773-3971

Evenflo Juvenile Products
P.O. Box 190
Ravenna, OH 44266
(216) 296-3465

Family Life Products
Box 541
Dennis, MA 02638
(617) 385-9109

F & H Baby Products Co.
P.O. Box 2228
Evansville, IN 47714
(812) 479-8485

The First Years (see Kiddie
    Products, Inc.)

Fisher-Price
620 Girard Ave.
East Aurora, NY 14052-
    1879
(800) 828-1440

Gerber Products
445 State St.
Fremont, MI 49412
(616) 928-2000

Gerico, Inc.
P.O. Box 33755
Denver, CO 80233
(303) 457-0926

Glenco
108 Fairway
Northvale, NJ

Graco Children's Products
Elverson, PA 19520
(215) 286-5951

Health Care Products, Inc.
P.O. Box 26221
Denver, CO 80226
(303) 337-4198

Hedstrom Company
P.O. Box 432
Bedford, PA 15522-0432
(814) 623-9041

Jagco Enterprises
P.O. Box 1541
Canoga Park, CA 91304
(818) 888-1967

Johnson & Johnson
Baby Products Company
220 Centennial Ave.
Piscataway, NJ 08854
(800) 526-3324

Just for Kids!
Winterbrook Way
Meredith, NH 03253
(603) 279-7031

Kewaunee Equipment
P.O. Box 224
Kewaunee, WI 54216
(414) 388-3232

Kiddie Products, Inc.
One Kiddie Dr.
Avon, MA 02322
(800) 225-0382 or
(617) 588-1220

Kindergard Corp.
14822 Venture Dr.
Dallas, TX 75234
(800) 527-2338

Kolcraft Products, Inc.
3455 W. 31st Pl.
Chicago, IL 60623
(312) 247-4494

Leading Lady
24000 Mercantile Rd.
Beachwood, OH 44122
(216) 464-5490

Life Manufacturing Co.
20 Meridian St.
East Boston, MA 02128
(617) 569-1200

Little Tikes
2180 Barlow Road
Hudson, OH 44236
(216) 650-3000

Lopuco, Ltd.
1615 Old Annapolis Rd.
Woodbine, MD 21797
(301) 489-4949

Marshall Electronics
600 Barclay Blvd.
Lincolnshire, IL 60069
(800) 323-1482
In Illinois: (312) 634-6300

The Mary Jane Co.
3015 Glendale Blvd.
Los Angeles, CA 90039
(213) 877-7166

Medallion Juvenile
  Products
6973 Consolidated Way
San Diego, CA 92121
(800) 421-2423

Medi-Aid Corporation
P.O. Box 4794
Englewood, CO 80155
(800) 621-8385 ext. 228
or (303) 790-1655

Monterey Laboratories, Inc.
P.O. Box 15129
Las Vegas, NV 89114
(800) 637-9751 or
(702) 876-3888

North States Industries
3650 Fremont Ave. N.,
Minneapolis, MN 55412
(612) 522-6506

Nu-Line Industries, Inc.
P.O. Box 217
Suring, WI 54174
(800) 558-7300 or
(414) 842-2141

Pansy Ellen Products, Inc.
P.O. Box 720274
Atlanta, GA 30358
(404) 448-2526

Perego Products, Inc.
455 Barell Ave.
Carlstadt, NJ 07072
(201) 935-5055

Practical Parenting
Dept. 18326-B
Minnetonka Blvd.
Deephaven, MN 55391
(612) 475-1505

Pride-Trimble Corporation
539 Rosecrans Ave.
Gardena, CA 90248
(213) 770-6382

Questor Juvenile Furniture
(*see* Evenflo Juvenile
   Furniture Company)

Red Calliope & Assoc., Inc.
13003 S. Figuero
Los Angeles, CA 90061
(213) 516-6100

Reliance Products Corp.
108 Mason St.
Woonsocket, RI 02895
(401) 769-8230

Sandbox Industries
P.O. Box 477
Tenafly, NJ 07670
(201) 567-5696

Sanitoy, Inc.
P.O. Box 2167
Fitchburg, MA 01420-2167
(800) 343-6032 or
(617) 345-7571

Sassy Inc.
3170 Doolittle Dr.
Northbrook, IL 60062
(312) 441-8680

Schaper Manufacturing Co.
P.O. Box 1426
Minneapolis, MN 55440
(612) 540-0511

Simmons Juvenile Products
613 E. Beacon Ave.
New London, WI 54961
(414) 982-2140

Snugli, Inc.
1212 Kerr Gulch
Evergreen, CO 80439
(303) 526-0131

Strolee of California
P.O. Box 5786
Rancho Dominguez, CA
   90224-5786
(213) 639-9300

Tailored Baby, Inc.
520 Library St.
San Fernando, CA 91342
(818) 365-9861

Tamara Dee, Inc.
9057 Greenwood Ave. N.
Seattle, WA 98103
(206) 784-8009

Tommee Tippee/Playskool
108 Fairway Court
Northvale, NJ 07647
(201) 767-0900

Tomy Corporation
P.O. Box 6252
Carson, CA 90749
(213) 549-2721

Welsh Company
1535 S. 8th St.
St. Louis, MO 63104
(314) 231-8822

The Wallace, Davis Co.
P.O. Box 841
Cheshire, CT 06410
(203) 272-1984

Williamsburg/Connor
Div. of Connor Forest Ind.
330 Fourth St.
P.O. Box 847
Wausau, WI 54401
(715) 842-0511

PRODUCT INDEX